TOTAL ACOUSTIC GUITAR

TIPS & TECHNIQUES FOR BECOMING A WELL-ROUNDED PLAYER

BY ANDREW DUBROCK

T0078928

PLAYBACK+
Speed • Pitch • Balance • Loop

To access audio visit:
www.halleonard.com/mylibrary

Enter Code
3020-4626-1100-7120

ISBN 978-1-4234-7012-0

HAL•LEONARD®

Visit Hal Leonard Online at
www.halleonard.com

Contact Us:
Hal Leonard
7777 West Bluemound Road
Milwaukee, WI 53213
Email: info@halleonard.com

In Europe contact:
Hal Leonard Europe Limited
Distribution Centre, Newmarket Road
Bury St Edmunds, Suffolk, IP33 3YB
Email: info@halleonardeurope.com

In Australia contact:
Hal Leonard Australia Pty. Ltd.
4 Lentara Court
Cheltenham, Victoria, 3192 Australia
Email: info@halleonard.com.au

TABLE OF CONTENTS

TITLE	PAGE	TRACK #

ABOUT THE AUTHOR

Andrew DuBrock is an independent music consultant who lives in Portland, Oregon. He has worked as an editor, transcriber, engraver, and author for Hal Leonard Corporation and served as Music Editor for *Acoustic Guitar*, *Strings*, and *Play Guitar!* magazines for seven years. A sampling of his instructional works include *Best of Lennon and McCartney for Acoustic Guitar* (DVD) and *Rock/Pop Guitar Songs for Dummies* (book/audio). His independent acoustic pop/rock CD, *DuBrock*, can be found at www.dubrock.net and www.cdbaby.com.

If you have comments or questions about this book, you can reach Andrew at *adubrock@comcast.net*.

ABOUT THE AUDIO

Most of the music examples in this book are performed on the accompanying audio tracks. When an example includes audio, you'll see the following track icon near the upper right-hand corner of the example:

Track 12

Many tracks include more than one example. In this case, the track icon is listed along with a time code indicating precisely where in the track that example appears (in minutes and seconds [00:00]):

Track 12
00:00

When more than one instrument appears on the recording, the featured part is always panned hard right. To hear this part alone, set your balance knob hard right; to hear the backing tracks alone, set your balance knob hard left.

INTRODUCTION

Total Acoustic Guitar is for everyone wanting to become a more complete acoustic guitarist—a *total* player. With complete sections devoted to rhythm, lead, and fingerpicking, you can hone in on whatever skill set you feel is lacking. If you want to become the total acoustic guitarist, you'll want to master every section.

This book is designed to get you "over the hump"—from a beginner level player to an intermediate or advanced player. If you've played guitar for a year-and-a-half or so and are looking to increase your skills, this book's a perfect companion for you as your guitar journey unfolds. If you've played for a bit longer, you can skim the more basic lessons for review, if necessary, and still find plenty of new material later on in each section. More experienced guitarists may learn a trick or two or may benefit from re-exploring techniques they haven't in quite some time. So, let's pick up our guitars and start our journey towards becoming *total* acoustic guitarists!

TUNING NOTES

Track 1

SECTION I:
GETTING STARTED
(A Review of the Basics)

Total Acoustic Guitar assumes you've played at least a little guitar (about a year to a year and a half), but this section is included to review the basics and fill in any gaps you may have in your basic skill set. Though we use the word "review," you may find chords or strumming ideas that you haven't come across in your travels, so it's worth reading through the chapters even if you consider yourself an advanced beginner.

If this is your first time playing guitar, this section may move a little quickly. If you stick with it, however, you should be able to pick up all you need to know before moving on to the more advanced sections (**Rhythm**, **Fingerpicking**, and **Lead**).

Try it out, move ahead if you want to, and make sure to *have fun!*

CHAPTER 1: BASIC CHORDS

OPEN-POSITION CHORDS

Open-position chords are the ones played down at the nut of your guitar (the "nut" is that piece of bone or plastic at the end of your guitar's fretboard, near the tuners). You may know some—or even all—of these chords. If you do, scan through and review them, play each one, and make sure you have your fingers in the right places. You may even find a few you've never seen before; spend extra time on these, and play through the chord-changing exercises before you move on. Ironing out chord-changing issues *before* you try playing more difficult parts means fewer mistakes in the long run. If you don't do this in the beginning, you may actually *ingrain the mistakes* into your chord changes, and it's much more difficult to *unlearn* those mistakes than it is to learn things cleanly the first time.

MAJOR CHORDS

Here are the open-position *major chords*. We're not going to worry about what a major chord is right now, but if you'd like to know more, see the appendix on **Chord Theory**. Fret-hand fingerings are shown at the bottom of each diagram. Place each finger on the string, making sure to bend it at the knuckles to form an upside-down "U" (you *don't* want your fingers to flatten their pads on the fret with the first knuckle bending backwards).

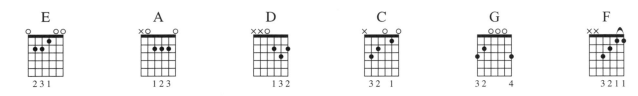

To help your fret-hand fingers nail these chords shapes more efficiently, let's practice changing between chord shapes. We'll start with a G–C chord change. Strum the G chord once or twice slowly, switch to the C chord, strum it a few times, and continue going back and forth between the two until you feel comfortable moving from one to the other.

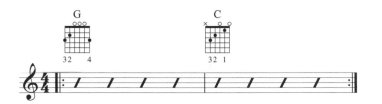

Track 2
00:00

Once you're comfortable moving between the C and G chords, try the E–A chord change below:

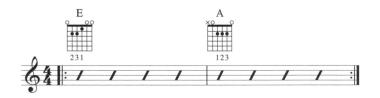

Track 2
00:15

Now, let's move on to an A–D chord progression:

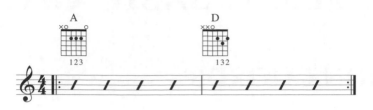

Track 2
00:29

Finally, let's incorporate that F chord into our repertoire, with a C–F chord progression. The F chord is the toughest chord so far, because it uses a two-string barre. A *barre* occurs when one finger frets more than one string by lying flat across the fretboard. In this case, flatten your index finger so that the fleshy part between the tip and first joint covers the top two strings.

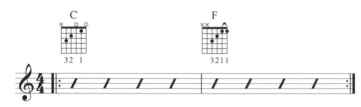

Track 2
00:43

MINOR CHORDS

Now let's look at open-position *minor chords*. (Again, we're not worrying about the theory behind these chords; if you'd like more on that, see the appendix on **Chord Theory**.)

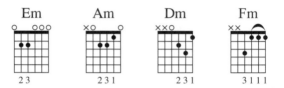

Moving back and forth between two chords is always a good drill, too. Just like you did with the major chords, try moving back and forth between two chords at a time. This time, you get to pick which chords to use together—but make sure to practice them *all*!

DOMINANT SEVENTH CHORDS

Now that we've re-acquainted ourselves with the major and minor chords, let's move on to *seventh chords*. Here, we're looking at *dominant seventh chords*, which are built from a major triad with a minor seventh interval on top (for more on the theory behind these chords, see the appendix on **Chord Theory**). Dominant seventh chords are a staple in almost every style of music, from jazz to pop, and especially in blues. Here are the dominant seventh chords in open position:

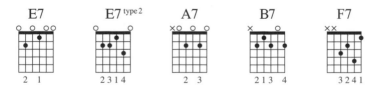

Notice the two fingerings for E7, and how they sound slightly different because the defining seventh note is in a higher place in the second version. Just as we did for the other chord types, practice changing between all of these chords before moving on to the minor seventh chords.

MINOR SEVENTH CHORDS

Minor seventh chords are built by placing a minor seventh interval on top of a minor triad. Minor seventh chords are popular in many styles, especially jazz, but also in pop and blues. Here are the minor seventh chords in open position:

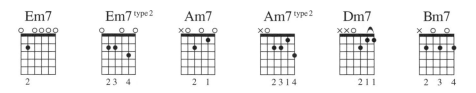

Here, you'll notice there are two fingerings for both the Em7 and Am7 chords. Though one may be easier than the other, make sure to learn them both; each one may sound better in different circumstances. Again, practice changing between these chords—and the other chord types we've looked at—before moving on to the major seventh chords.

MAJOR SEVENTH CHORDS

Major seventh chords are built by placing a major seventh interval on top of a major triad. Major seventh chords are less common than dominant or minor seventh chords, but they're used extensively in jazz and are also found in pop and blues.

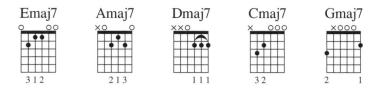

BARRE CHORDS

Barre chords get their name from a finger that lies (or "barres") across multiple strings. Most barre chords don't use any open strings. While barre chords are tougher to master (those pesky barres are hard to hold down), they have a huge payoff, because they open up the *entire* fretboard; each shape can be moved to any fret, so one shape can essentially play every letter name, from A to G.

MAJOR AND MINOR BARRES

We'll look at two barre chord shapes for each chord type; one shape has its root note (the letter name of the chord) on the fifth string, and the other has its root on the sixth string. Here's an E-shape barre chord, with the root on the sixth string:

Can you guess why it's called an E-shape barre chord? It's because the E chord shape is part of the chord—the part played with your second, third, and fourth fingers. Try re-fingering an open E chord using your second, third, and fourth fingers, and you'll see what I mean.

If you're learning this chord for the first time, take it slowly. This one's difficult for everyone to master. There's often an urge to press too hard with your index finger, but once you get the hang of it, you'll realize it has more to do with a small amount of pressure *in the right places*. For instance, you don't need to worry about pressing the strings down behind notes fretted by other fingers—you really only have to worry about keeping the first, fifth, and sixth strings pressed down with that index finger.

If you can't get all the strings to sound, or if some are buzzing on the frets, try moving your index finger closer to the fret or try rolling your index finger inward or outwards slightly so different portions of it contact the strings.

It's easier to practice this shape between the third and sixth frets, since the wider fret spacing at the nut make the reaches harder and the strings' higher distance from the fretboard up the neck make holding the chord harder up there. Once you have this shape down, you can play *any* major chord with this one shape:

Major Barre Chords on the Sixth String

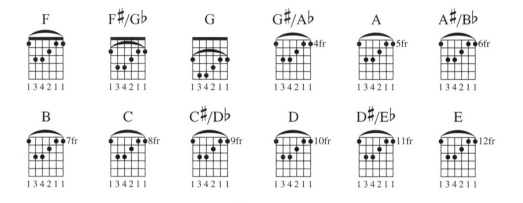

Here's the other major barre-chord shape—an A-shape barre with the root on the fifth string:

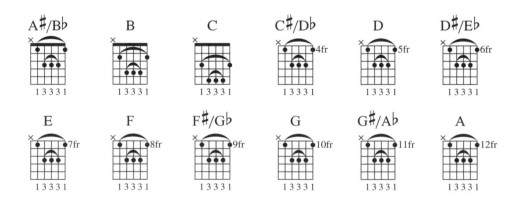

In some ways, this shape is even harder than the E-shape barre chord, because bending your ring finger to allow that first string to ring through is near impossible for many folks. But I'll let you in on a little secret: a good number of us don't play that first string at all. Instead, let your index or ring finger lightly touch the first string just enough to dampen it so it doesn't sound. The chord still sounds great even without this string ringing.

Once you have this shape down, you can also play any major chord with this shape:

Major Barre Chords on the Fifth String

Now let's look at minor barre chords. Here is the Em-shape barre chord:

And here's the Am-shape barre chord:

If you move these same shapes up the neck, you can play every minor chord with these shapes, just as we did with the major chords.

SEVENTH CHORD BARRES

Now, let's take a look at seventh chord barres. Here are two variations on an E7-shape barre chord:

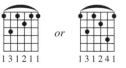

Either one of these shapes will work fine; you may find your own favorite, or you may find that each one works better in different situations.

Now let's look at the A7-shape barre chord:

Once you have the E7- and A7-shape barre chords down, remember that you can move them around to play every seventh chord, just like we did for the major chords.

The minor seventh barre chord shown below on the left is based on an Em7 shape. While this chord is occasionally used, the shape to the right is much more common. In the second shape, put your middle finger on the sixth string, rolling it slightly down to dampen the fifth string, and then barre from strings 2–5 with your ring finger. It's also common to continue the barre up through the first string, and this works fine, too.

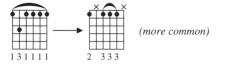

Here's the Am7-shape barre chord:

For major seventh chords, we again find two shapes with a root on the sixth string. The first shape is hardly used, though; most people opt for the shape at right, which uses all four fingers to grab the essential notes of this chord. Note that this isn't really a barre chord anymore, since no fingers actually barre across more than one string, but it's included here since it's a moveable form and is essentially used in place of the barre chord to the left.

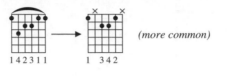

(more common)

Finally, here's the Amaj7-shape barre chord:

Remember that for all seventh chords, you can use the shapes shown here to play any letter name, just as we did for the major chords.

CHAPTER 2: BASIC STRUMMING

Before we look at more complicated strumming in **Chapter 3**, let's review a few basic strumming patterns. The pattern we'll start with is one strum on each beat. For each quarter note, strum downward (towards the floor), then move your hand back up so you can strum the next quarter note with another downstroke:

QUARTER NOTE STRUMS

Track 3
00:00

Make sure to count along "1, 2, 3, 4" as you play these strums, and tap your foot evenly on the floor to help get your strums in a steady rhythm. Next up is the eighth-note strum pattern. Count along again, this time saying, "1-&, 2-&, 3-&, 4-&." For the eighth notes, play both down- and upstrokes. You'll play a downstroke on every beat—just as you did in the previous example—but you'll now play an upstroke for every "&."

EIGHTH-NOTE STRUMS

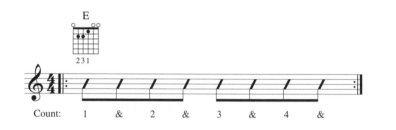

Track 3
00:09

Try to make the motion as natural as possible. Your hand moves constantly in a down-up-down-up motion and should feel like a pendulum moving up and down. This kind of motion should eventually feel like walking, running, or any other natural rhythm your body performs without thinking.

Now let's start mixing quarter notes and eighth notes together. This is where the patterns start getting interesting! We'll start off with a quarter note followed by eighth notes:

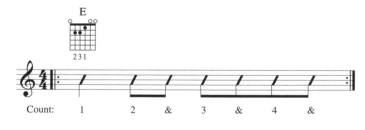

Track 3
00:19

Next, we'll play quarter notes on beats 1 *and* 3:

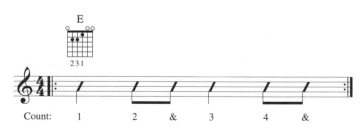

Track 3
00:28

Another common strum pattern includes a single bass note before strumming through the chord. Try this with an E chord by playing the low sixth string on beat 1 and following that up with strums on beats 2, 3, and 4.

> **TIP:** The bass-note strum example instructs you to strum through the top five strings, but don't worry about hitting *exactly* those strings. The most important part is to play the bass note and follow it up with strums through any part of the chord on the other beats.

BASS-NOTE STRUMS

Track 4
00:00

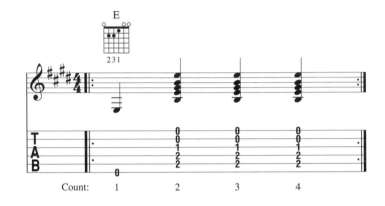

When you play bass-strum patterns like this, use the lowest note of the chord for your bass note. That means that for A or C chords, you'll play the fifth string as your bass note, and for D chords, you'll play the fourth string. Now let's try playing a bass-strum pattern that uses an A chord with eighth-note strums:

Track 4
00:08

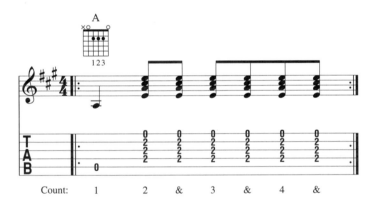

USING STRUM PATTERNS AND CHANGING CHORDS

Once you're comfortable playing a strum pattern on one chord, practice changing between chords and playing complete chord progressions. Here's a D–G–A chord progression to get you started:

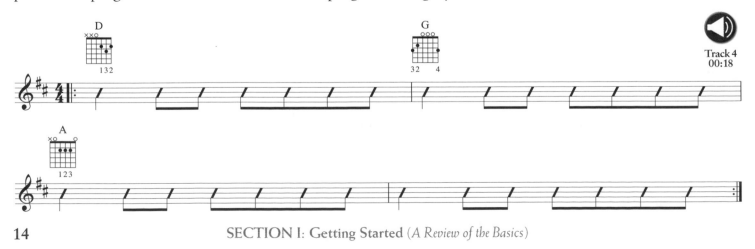

Track 4
00:18

Try this out with many different chords and progressions. Also try switching between strum patterns to get yourself comfortable playing any pattern at any time. (In complete songs, it's not a good idea to switch strum patterns too often, or the rhythm might not sound even anymore.) Here's an A–D–E progression:

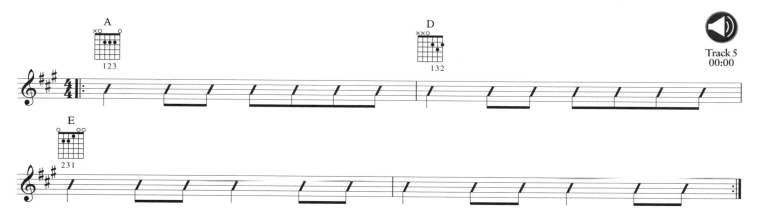

Track 5
00:00

TIP: EASIER CHORD CHANGES

Here's a trick *every* guitarist uses to make their chord changes easier: Start switching chords a little early and strum the top few open strings while you get your fingers into place for the next chord. If you strum the open strings for only the last eighth note of a chord, it doesn't sound too bad. This allows you to be firmly in place for the downbeat of the next chord. Listen very closely to some of your favorite songs and you'll be surprised at how often this happens. Here's how it sounds in an E–A–B7 chord progression:

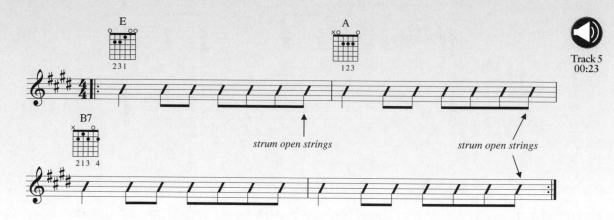

Track 5
00:23

strum open strings

strum open strings

STRUM PATTERNS IN POPULAR SONGS

Eighth-Note Strums: "Learning to Fly"–Tom Petty and the Heartbreakers, "Best of My Love"–The Eagles

Quarter-/Eighth-Note Combinations: "(Don't Go Back to) Rockville"–R.E.M., "Waterloo Sunset"–The Kinks, "Band on the Run"–Wings

Bass-Note Strums: "New Slang"–The Shins, "Rocky Raccoon"–The Beatles

CHAPTER 3:
ALTERNATE BASS STRUMMING

Alternate bass strumming takes the bass-strum patterns from **Chapter 2** one step further, adding an *alternate* bass note every other time. To see how this works, let's start off with a bass-strum pattern on an E chord:

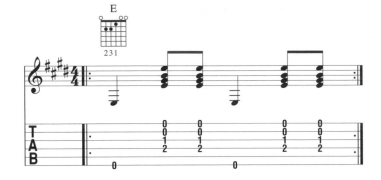

Track 6
00:00

Now, let's alternate bass notes between the sixth and fifth strings of the E chord, like this:

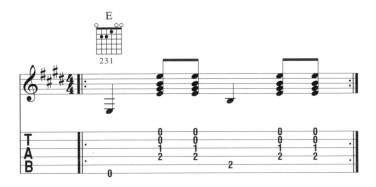

Track 6
00:10

As a general rule, use the lowest note of a chord for your first bass note and alternate that with a bass note one string away—either on the next higher string or next *lower* string. Let's try this on an A chord:

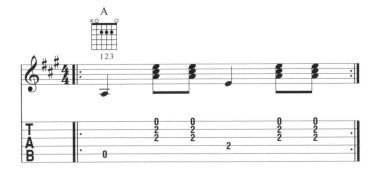

Track 6
00:19

Note how we went *up* a string here for the second bass note, just like we did for the E chord. But, you can also go *down* one string on the A chord, like this:

Track 6
00:29

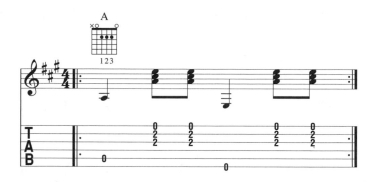

For a D chord, we could try this:

Track 7
00:00

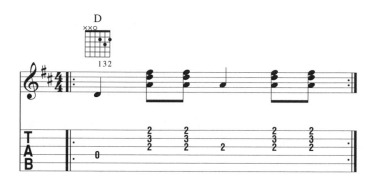

But notice how that second bass note sounds a bit high. You can certainly use this alternate-bass pattern, but going down to the lower string is more popular on a D chord:

Track 7
00:10

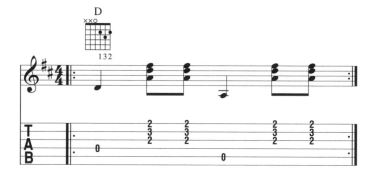

Now let's try a C chord:

Track 7
00:20

CHAPTER 3: Alternate Bass Strumming

Notice how this one sounds a little different because that fourth string bass note is the 3rd of the chord instead of the 5th. (If you're not sure what the 3rd or 5th of a chord is, see the appendix on **Chord Theory**.) The 3rd sounds nice as a bass note, but if you prefer hearing that 5th, you can skip up to the third string to play the alternate-bass pattern like this:

Track 7
00:30

Again, this note sounds a little high, so it's very common to go *down* one string for the C chord. To do this, though, you'll need to fret the third fret. So lift your ring finger off of its bass note and move it down to the sixth string. When you repeat and go back to the original bass note, you'll have to move your finger back up to the fifth string. This may feel difficult at first, but over time it will feel like a natural rocking pattern between the two strings.

Alternatively, you can re-finger the C chord, using your pinky for the C note on string 5 and your third finger for the G note on string 6, as shown in the alternate chord diagram.

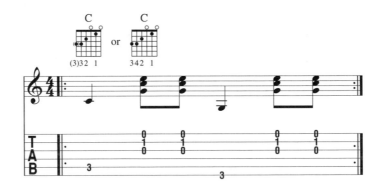

Track 8
00:00

The G chord is similar to a C chord; if you play an alternate bass-strum pattern by going up one string, you get the 3rd in the bass again:

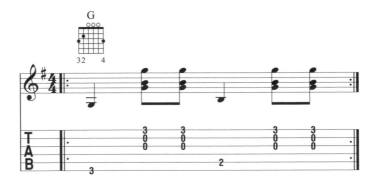

Track 8
00:09

Again, if you prefer that 5th, skip up one more string for a fourth-string bass note:

Track 8
00:20

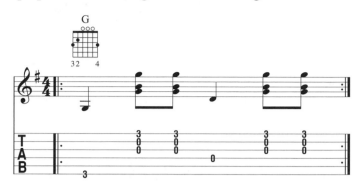

Now let's try a complete chord progression! This may sound familiar to you, since it's similar to the one in Crosby, Stills, Nash, and Young's "Teach Your Children." If you know how to play any other songs, try applying alternate bass/strums to them to see how they sound.

Track 9

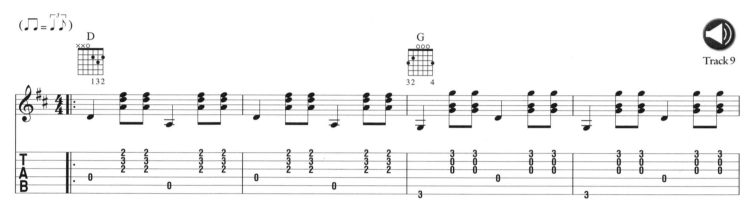

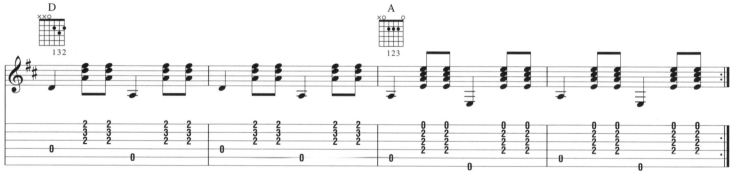

SONGS WITH ALTERNATE BASS STRUMMING

- "Teach Your Children"–Crosby, Stills, Nash & Young

- "Swinging Doors"–Merle Haggard

- "Adrift" (Rhythm part)–Jack Johnson

- "Long Road"–Patty Griffin

CHAPTER 4: WALKING BASS LINES

Playing chords is the most basic way to back up a song, but playing *only* chords song after song can sound monotonous—especially if you're not playing with other instruments. One of the most common ways to dress up strum patterns is to add *walking bass lines*. In this chapter, we'll add walking bass lines to alternate-bass strum patterns, but you can use walking bass lines with any strum pattern you like.

WALKING BASS LINES JOIN CHORDS

Walking bass lines add interest to your chord progressions by injecting some single notes between chords. Let's dive in and start by learning a bass line that walks into G:

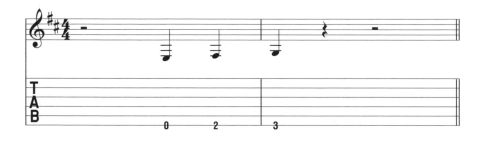

Now let's play the walking bass line and follow it up with alternate-bass strumming on the G chord:

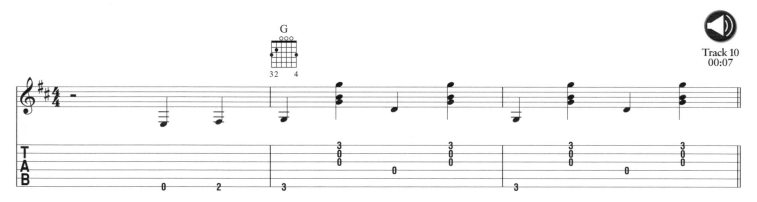

To see how this works as a transition between chords, play a D chord for a measure and a half and then throw in the walking bass line followed by the G chord, like this:

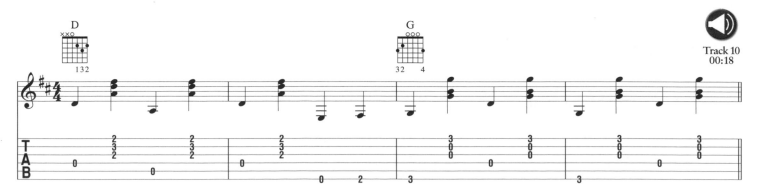

Now let's try walking from G back to D:

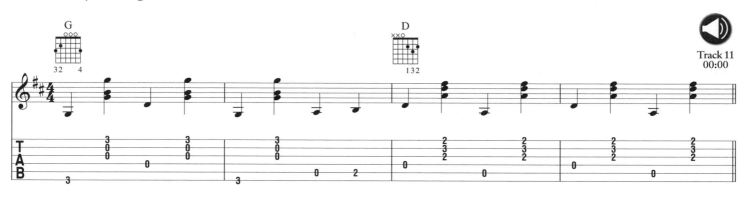

Now let's learn two more walking bass lines at the same time. The first one joins D to A, and the next one brings us from A back to D. Try repeating this until you get the hang of it.

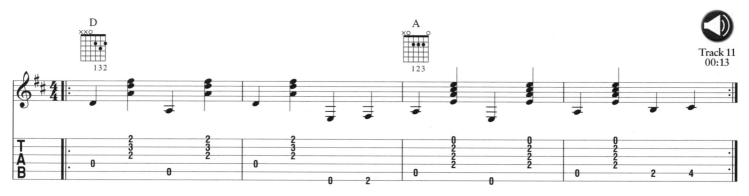

At this point, we're ready to try our walking bass lines in the chord progression from **Chapter 3**:

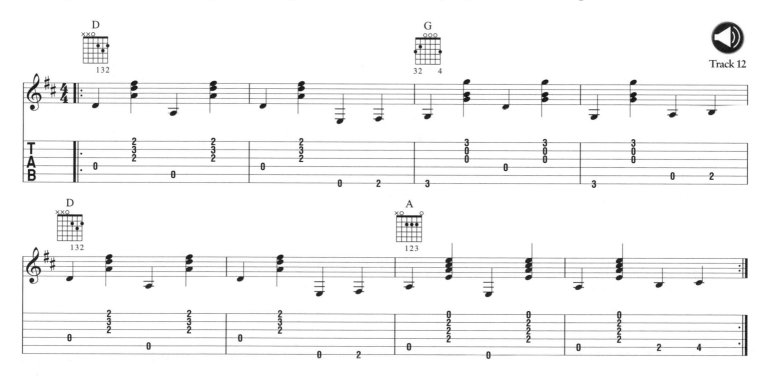

USE SCALES OR YOUR EAR TO CREATE WALKING BASS LINES

So far, we've learned a few walking bass lines that work between chords when playing a song in the key of D major. But when you switch to another key, not all of these bass lines will work. For instance, check out the walking bass lines in the next chord progression, which is in the key of C major.

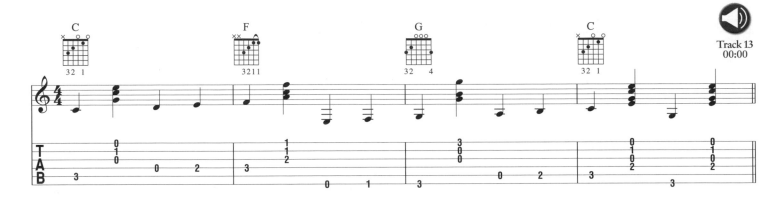

We haven't seen a walking bass line—or an alternating bass—for an F chord yet. But since it's new, it's not necessarily unexpected. The unexpected part of the above example is the walking bass line into G because it's different from the bass line we've been playing into a G chord. Instead of playing the second fret (which is an F♯ note), we're playing the *first* fret (F♮).

You can build these scales with a little music theory knowledge (see the gray box "Scales and Walking Bass Lines"), but you can also rely on your ear to tell you what works. Play the previous example through with an F♯ note (the second fret) instead of the F (first fret) on the walk up to G, and you'll see that this just *sounds* wrong in the context of the chord progression.

SCALES AND WALKING BASS LINES

The secret behind these walking bass lines is that you build them from the scale associated with the song's key. This may sound mighty complicated, but it's not. The C–F–C–G progression is in the key of C major, so we're using notes from a C major scale. If the song was in G major, we'd use the G major scale to construct our bass lines; and if the song was in the key of D minor, we'd use the D minor scale for our bass lines. (To learn how to construct major and minor scales, see **Chapters 19** and **20**.)

TIP: Rock on the F chord alternate bass like you do with a C chord—picking up that ring finger and moving it down to play the alternate bass note. For the F chord, rock between the fourth and fifth strings, instead of the fifth and sixth strings (like you do with a C chord).

ADD PASSING NOTES TO FILL OUT BASS LINES

Sometimes you'll have a bass run that ends too early, either because you don't have enough notes between two chords, or because you want to start your walking bass line at a different time. For instance, if you wanted to start your walk from C to F earlier, you'd end up on the F chord *before* the next measure:

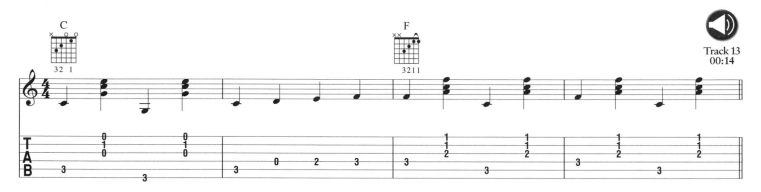

While this sounds OK, that arrival to the F chord is a little less exciting because the bass note gets there *before* the downbeat of the measure. To fill things out, we'll insert a *passing note* to elongate that bass run. A "passing note" is basically a note added between two scale or chord tones—or, more simply, any note inserted between two notes in your walking bass line. In our souped-up bass line below, the passing note is E♭.

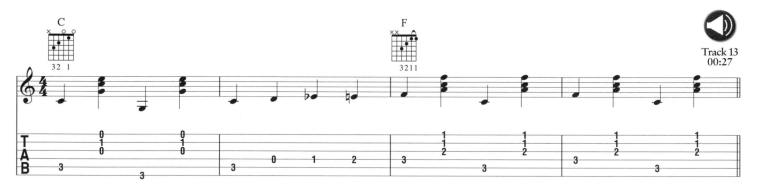

Let's try one more bass line with a passing note. This time we'll walk from C to the G chord.

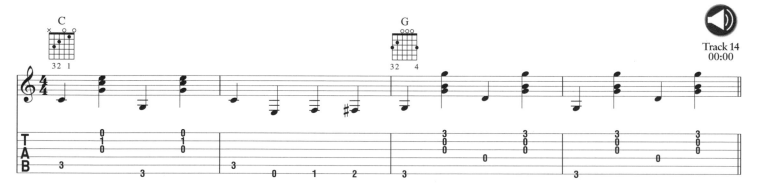

If you're wondering why that second fret (F♯) sounds OK here but not earlier, it's because in this context, it's inserted as a passing note between the first and third frets. If you play the open E string and jump up to that second fret, it will sound strange, but when it's carefully sandwiched between two notes as a passing note, it sounds fine.

WALKING BASS LINES WITH CHORDS IN BETWEEN

For a slightly different sound, you can also alternate the notes of your walking bass line with chord strums. Try this out moving from C to F:

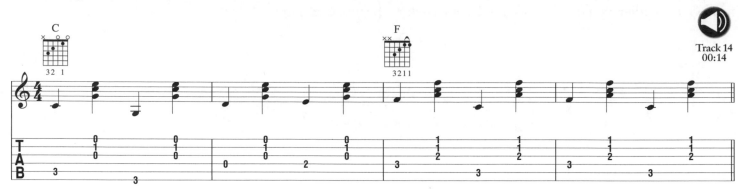

Walking bass lines like this can be tricky to pull off, since you'll have to keep fretting some of the previous chord while also playing those walking bass notes. Try this technique out on some of the other walking bass lines you learned earlier in this chapter, then try adding walking bass lines to songs you already know how to play.

> ### Songs with Walking Bass Lines
> • "Between the Bars" (Chorus)–Elliott Smith
> • "I Walk the Line"–Johnny Cash
> • "Friend of the Devil"–Grateful Dead

SECTION II:
RHYTHM

Rhythm is the foundation of all guitar music. Without a solid rhythm, there would be nothing to play lead over. In fact, you don't *need* lead guitar for a song to work, but you *do* need rhythm guitar to play almost everything. Unfortunately, many guitarists completely forget about rhythm, instead focusing on lead playing since they think it will garner more attention and/or be more rewarding. But rhythm guitar playing can be a lot of fun and rewarding, too. And solid rhythm translates to better lead playing, as well; there's nothing worse than a lead guitarist who can't feel the rhythm! In this section, we'll work on developing our rhythm chops in a variety of ways—from syncopated grooves, to chunking power chord rhythms, to rhythmic fills.

CHAPTER 5: SYNCOPATION

Steady rhythms hold a song together, but a song isn't fun unless it *grooves*. So how do acts like the Rolling Stones get those funky rhythms that groove? They use *syncopation*. The word "syncopation" may trip up your tongue the first time you say it, and though it may sound like some arcane scientific concept or a digestive symptom we'd better not get into, it's really just a fancy music word meaning to accent the weak beats.

BASIC SYNCOPATION

To get a sense of how syncopation works, let's look at the most basic strong and weak beats in a measure of music. When you play a pop or rock song, usually the bass drum hits on beats 1 and 3, like this:

Track 15
00:00

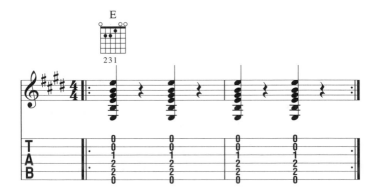

Those are the most basic strong beats in a measure. So, if you simply play on beats 2 and 4, where the snare normally hits, you're playing the most basic form of syncopation:

Track 15
00:11

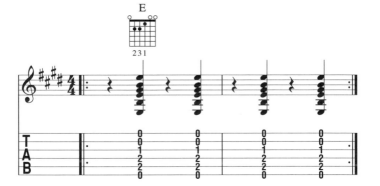

Many reggae tunes use this basic syncopation with small chord shapes up the neck. In the following example, just strum through the top strings of an A barre chord in fifth position or fret just the top three strings with your index and middle fingers, making sure to dampen those lower strings with the rest of your strumming or picking hand. Try quickly damping the chord after you strum to get that reggae sound:

Track 15
00:22

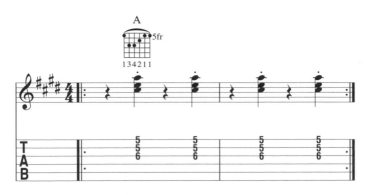

ADD SYNCOPATION BY LEAVING OUT STRUMS

So far, we've played syncopations with quarter notes. Now let's try syncopating some eighth-note strum patterns. We'll start with a steady eighth-note pattern:

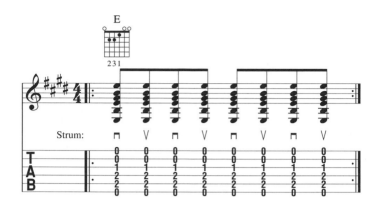

Notice the symbols in the music that tell you which way to strum: ⊓ for downstroke and ∨ for upstroke. When you're playing eighth notes, all of the strums on each beat are stronger than the ones *between* each beat (the *offbeats*: where you count "&" between each number). All of the strong beats are played with downstrokes, so leaving out a downstroke will create a syncopated strum pattern, like this:

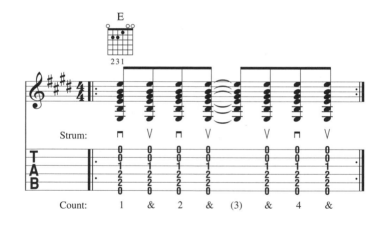

TIP: COUNT THE BEATS AND KEEP YOUR STRUMMING HAND MOVING!

Don't worry if you have trouble playing these syncopated strums. Slow things down and count along as you play, making sure to count *every* beat and offbeat: "1-&, 2-&, 3-&, 4-&." Hearing each beat subdivided like that helps you hear and feel which beats you need to strum on. When you're playing sixteenth-note patterns, you count "1-ee-&-ah, 2-ee-&-ah..."

While you focus on counting and when to strum, make sure to *keep your strumming hand moving* in a constant down-up motion (often called *pendulum strumming*). Just let your arm move a little away from the guitar for the strums where you're not supposed to play and bring it back for the strums you do want to make. This purposeful "missing" when strumming is referred to as a "ghost stroke."

You can leave out any downstroke to create a syncopated strum pattern. In the next example, we'll leave out multiple downstrokes on beats 2, 3, and 4 for a very funky (and difficult!) strum pattern:

Track 16
00:15

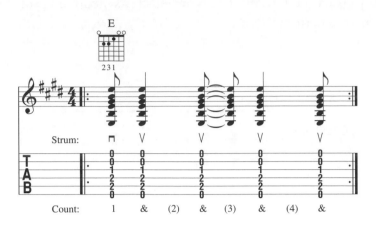

This is a difficult pattern to play, so don't worry if you have trouble. It helps to slow things down and count along for every eighth-note subdivision.

Now here's a pattern that leaves out *every* downstroke, making it an extremely syncopated example.

Track 16
00:22

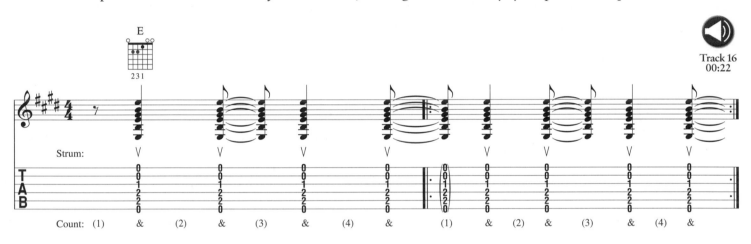

This one is a beast to play, and I'm including it mostly as a reference so you can really *hear* syncopation in action. In real-life songs, you'll rarely play a strum pattern that leaves out every strong beat. In fact, the best sounding strum patterns mix just the right amount of syncopation in. Here's an example reminiscent of the classic song "Twist and Shout." Note how the only syncopation happens at the end of the first measure, as the chords move through D to E7.

Track 17
00:00

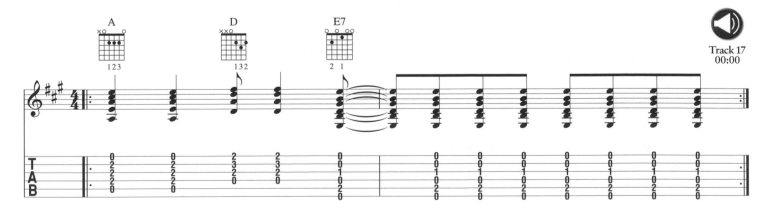

ACCENT WEAK BEATS WITH HEAVIER STRUMS

So far we've looked at how you can syncopate your strum patterns by using ghost strokes, or leaving out downstrokes, which naturally accents the upstrokes that you play. But you can also create syncopated strum patterns by playing those upstrokes louder than the surrounding downstrokes. This method adds a little extra bounce, and many acoustic pop-rock artists, and some traditional players (like Celtic guitarists), energize their syncopated strum patterns this way. Here's a syncopated strum pattern with accents on beats 1 and the "and" of beat 2. The sideways "V" under a strum indicates that you accent that strum:

Track 17
00:11

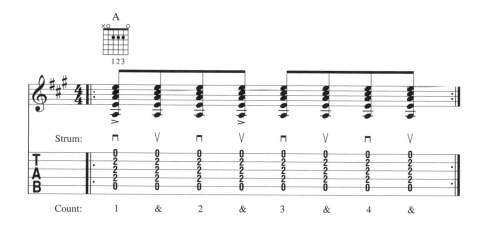

Now let's look at a longer progression that uses the same syncopation over a few chords. You might hear a Celtic musician backing up another instrument with this frenetic pattern. Notice how the first two accents highlight notes in groups of three, in contrast to the downbeats (which are in groups of two).

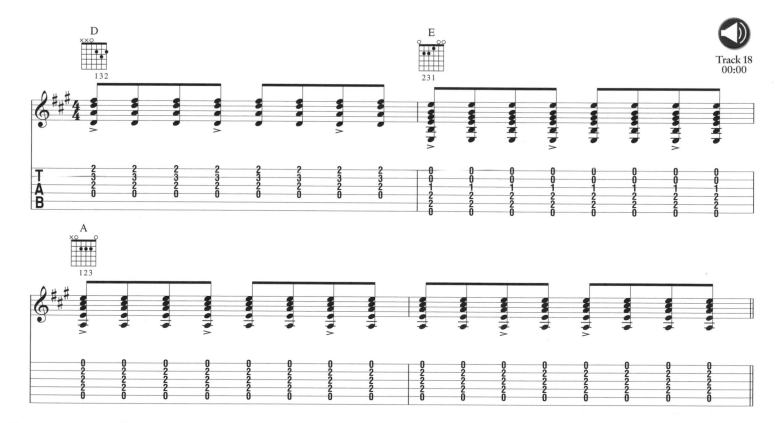

Track 18
00:00

A syncopated pulse that's popular across many genres is the "Bo Diddley" beat, which accents beats 1, the "and" of 2, and 4 in the first measure, and beats 2 and 3 in the second measure:

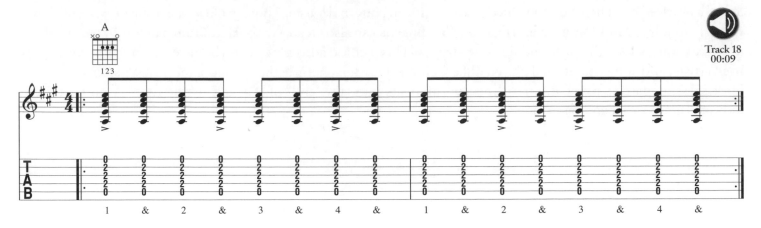

Remember that you can always choose between leaving out strums, accenting, or combining the two for your syncopated strums. Here's how the "Bo Diddley" beat looks when you leave out the strums:

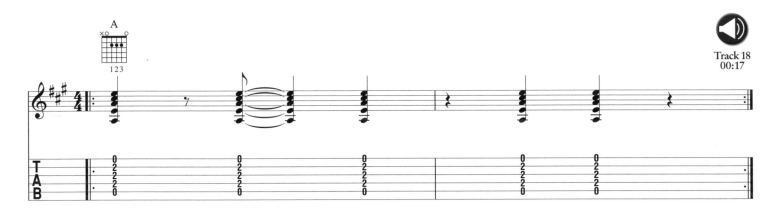

SONGS WITH SYNCOPATION

• "Me and Julio Down by the Schoolyard"–Paul Simon

• "Your Time Is Gonna Come"–Led Zeppelin

• "Pinball Wizard"–The Who

• "Not Fade Away"–Buddy Holly/The Rolling Stones

CHAPTER 6: POWER CHORDS

Power Chords sound like a semitruck using engine brakes when you play them on an electric guitar with a heavy dose of distortion, and that's probably where they got their name. But power chords also sound great on acoustic guitar. While most other chords are built from three or more notes, power chords are built from only two notes: the root and 5th of a scale. (See **Chapter 19: The Major Scale** if you want to know what the "root" and "5th" of a scale are.)

POWER CHORDS ON THE BOTTOM TWO STRINGS

Our first power chord is the lowest one you can play on the guitar—an E power chord:

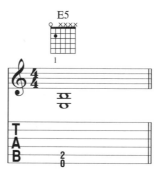

As you can see, it's an easy chord to wrap your fingers around—make that *one* finger! Hear how the chord sounds open, and note the chord label (E5), which denotes a power chord.

For our next power chord, we'll just slide this shape up one fret. Of course, you can't play that the same way, without any open strings, so pop your index finger down on the first fret of the sixth string and add your ring finger on the third fret of the fifth string, like this:

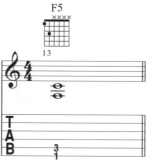

Once you have this shape under your fingers, you can play any power chord on the bottom two strings! Simply slide the shape up to any fret, and you've got another power chord. Here are all the power chords on the bottom two strings, from E5 all the way up to E♭5:

Power Chords on the Bottom Two Strings

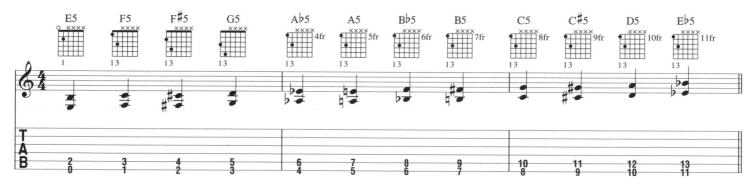

At this point, you can start playing riffs with these chords. Try this one, which may sound a little like a familiar Kinks tune:

POWER CHORD RIFF

Track 19
00:00

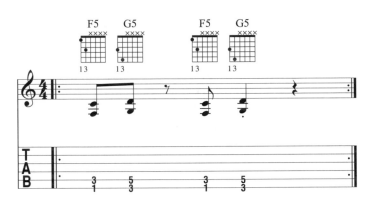

POWER CHORDS ON THE FOURTH AND FIFTH STRINGS

The great thing about power chords is that you can transfer their shape to most other string sets. Check out how the same E power-chord shape moved up one string set to the fourth and fifth strings makes an A power chord:

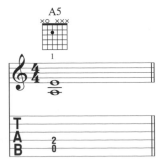

Of course, you can also transfer the F power-chord shape from the bottom two strings up to the fourth and fifth strings, where it becomes a B♭ power chord:

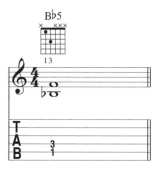

Now we can play all the power chords on the fourth and fifth strings, too:

Power Chords on the Fourth and Fifth Strings

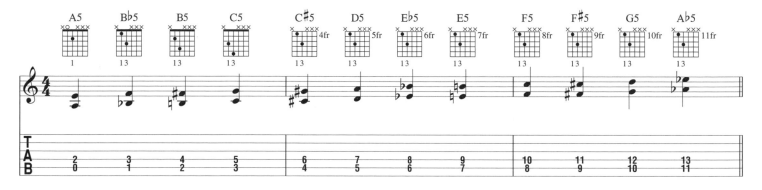

At this point, I'll let you in on a secret: knowing the power chords on these two string sets allows you to play almost anything on the same part of the neck. I'll show you how it works. Let's say we wanted to expand our Kinks-type riff a little, like this:

Power Chord Riff 2

Track 19
00:06

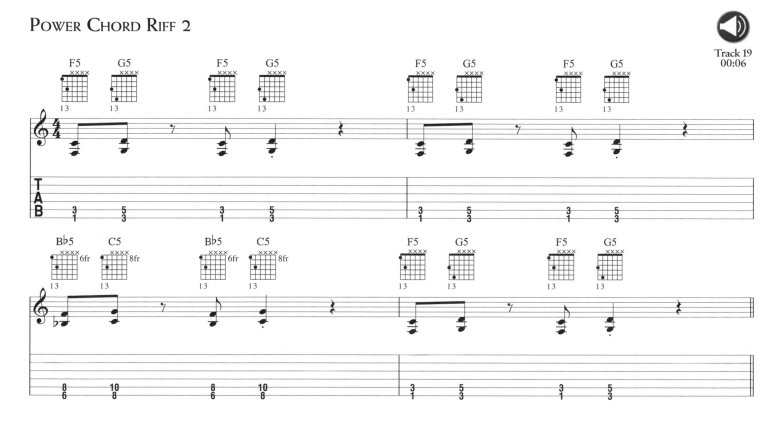

Everything's going fine for those first two measures, where you're just hanging out on the F and G power chords. But then in the third measure, you have to jump all the way up to the sixth and eighth frets! Even worse, in the next measure, you have to jump all the way back to the first fret from the eighth fret. If you're playing this riff at a fast clip, you might have trouble getting back down there in time. So here's where the shapes on our other strings come in handy. Let's just move that third measure up to shapes on the fourth and fifth strings, like this:

RIFF 2 ON MULTIPLE STRING SETS

Track 19
00:17

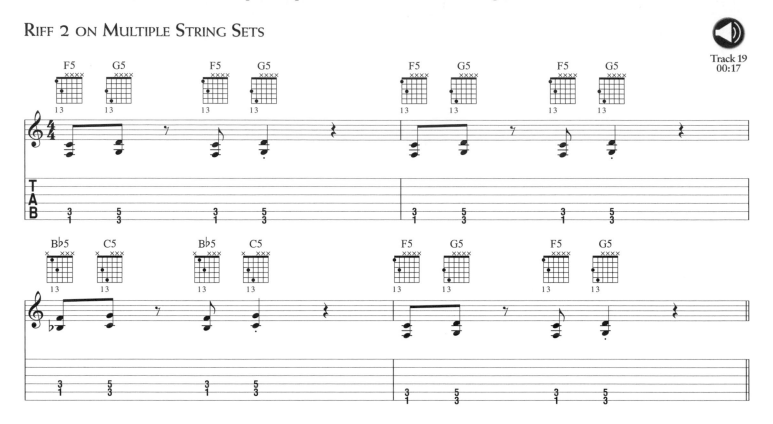

THREE-NOTE POWER CHORDS

If you want to fatten up your power chords, a common way is to add one more note on top. For the E and A power chords in open position, just use your middle finger on the lower string and add your ring finger to the second fret of the next highest string; for the moveable F and B♭ power-chord shapes, just place your pinky finger on the third fret of the next highest string:

THREE-NOTE POWER CHORDS ON BOTTOM THREE STRINGS

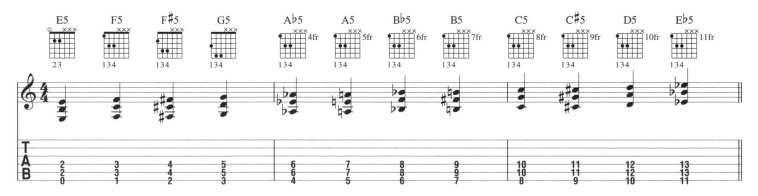

　　　SECTION II: Rhythm

Three-Note Power Chords on Third, Fourth, and Fifth Strings

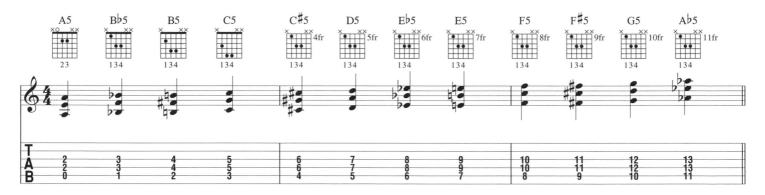

One fingering variation you can try out is to barre the top two strings of a three-note power chord. Just flatten your ring finger across the top two strings, like this:

Barred Power Chords

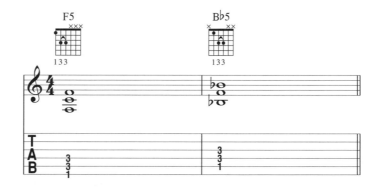

OPEN-POSITION POWER CHORDS

There are a few huge power chords you can play down in open position. Each one sounds great, but has its own unique quality. Try these out when you're playing in open position and want a larger-sounding power chord:

Root-Position Power Chords

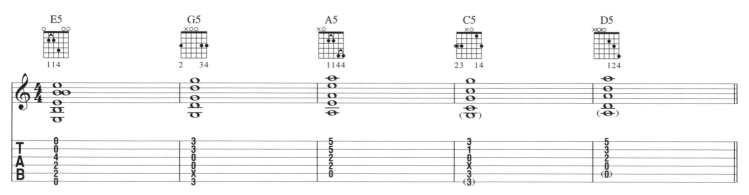

Some of these are tricky to grab, so take your time. The "X" in the tablature for the G and C power chords means that you need to dampen those strings. For the G power chord, do this by rolling your middle finger (which is on the sixth string) towards the fifth string and touch it just enough so it dampens the string and makes a "plunky" sound when you strum through it. For the C chord, roll your ring finger (which is on the fifth string) down to dampen the fourth string. The difficulty here is to keep a string fretted while dampening the next one. Be patient, keep trying, and you'll have it before you know it!

I've also indicated an extra note on the bottom for the C and D power chords in parentheses. You don't *need* these notes in those chords, but adding them can fatten up the sound even more.

Substituting these shapes for other power chords can really fill out your songs. But you don't need to use them for every possible chord. Sometimes one of these carefully placed sounds even better, like on this Who-style power chord riff:

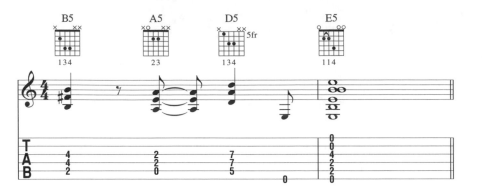

Track 19
00:28

PALM MUTING AND DOWNSTROKES

Now let's try out a complete song using power chords. We'll use the classic tune "House of the Rising Sun" to take our new chords for a spin. Before you dive in, check out the 6/8 time signature at the beginning of the song (the *time signature* is that stacked number at the left). This time signature has six beats, and you'll count a beat for each eighth note (for more on 6/8 time and time signatures, see the **Appendix**).

Notice how I use all downstrokes for the power-chord section in the first half. You'll see this happen all the time with power chords, because it gives them a heavier (and more-powerful) sound. Also notice the "P.M." note between tablature and notation, which stands for "palm mute." Use your pick-hand palm for palm muting by lightly laying the fleshy underside of your palm against the strings (the outside half of your palm which is closest to the floor and furthest from your thumb) near the bridge. You should hear a lightly-muted sound when you strum, but you should still be able to hear the notes of the chord. If the strings make a completely dampened "chukka" sound and you hear no notes, then let a little pressure off from your palm and/or move your palm back closer to the bridge.

Once you reach the E5 chord in measure 7, fret the whole chord, but only play the bottom strings for the first measure. Gradually get louder here (that's what that sideways "V" means, which is called a *crescendo* marking). Then, in the next measure, let your palm free of the muting and start strumming full "down-up-down/down-up-down" patterns. This strum pattern naturally accents beats 1 and 4, which are the strong beats in 6/8 time. If you have trouble with this strum pattern, try a strict "down-up" pattern instead.

HOUSE OF THE RISING SUN

Track 20

SECTION II: Rhythm

36

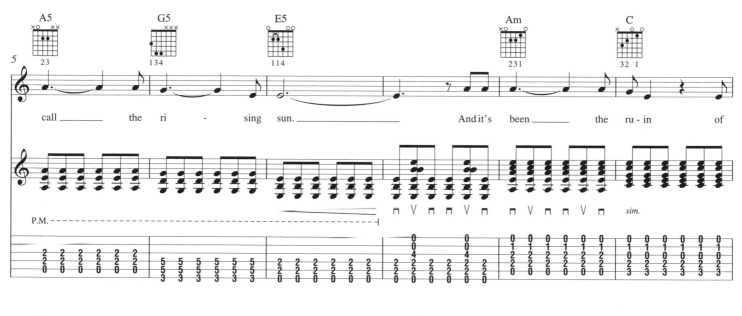

call _____ the ri - sing sun. _____ And it's been _____ the ru - in of

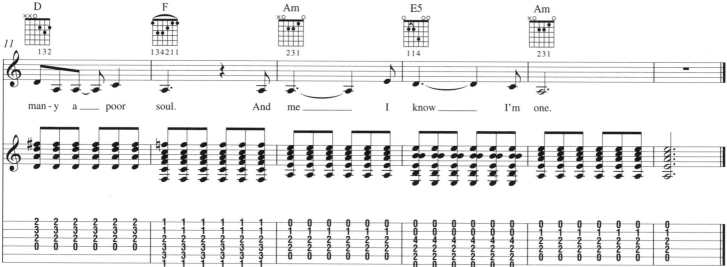

man - y a _____ poor soul. And me _____ I know _____ I'm one.

Southern American Folksong
Copyright © 2010 by HAL LEONARD CORPORATION
International Copyright Secured   All Rights Reserved

SONGS WITH POWER CHORDS

• "Behind Blue Eyes" (bridge)—The Who

• "You Really Got Me" (electric riff)—The Kinks

• "Smells Like Teen Spirit" (electric riff)—Nirvana

CHAPTER 7: SCRATCH RHYTHM

The term "scratch rhythm" might conjure up an image of a backyard jam: there's a cardboard guitar, a washtub bass, and over in the corner is someone scratching rhythms in the dirt with a stick. But we're not being quite that literal when we talk about *scratch rhythms*. Instead, scratch rhythm is a guitar technique that uses fret-hand damping to add a driving, percussive, and sometimes funky feel to your playing.

To play scratch rhythms, lay your fret-hand fingers across the strings so that you *completely* dampen them. Make sure you're not pressing down hard enough to fret notes; just apply enough pressure so that the strings are dampened. Then strum through the strings:

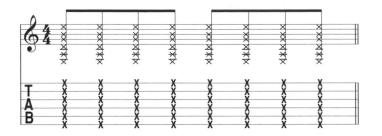

Track 21
00:00

You should hear a "chukka chukka" sound without actual notes. If you can make out notes, you're probably applying too much pressure; loosen your grip and try again.

Now try alternating between half a measure of scratch rhythm and half a measure of strums. For this exercise, it's helpful to get your hand in position to play the F chord by laying your first finger across the first fret, letting the rest of your fingers flatten alongside it. Then, when the F chord happens, pop your middle, ring, and pinky fingers into place and grab the chord. After the chord, quickly loosen your grip and dampen the strings again.

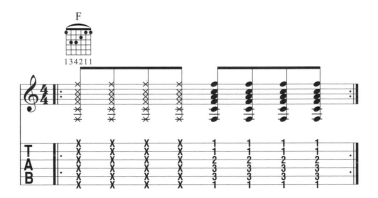

Track 21
00:05

Now let's try alternating every two eighth notes, like this:

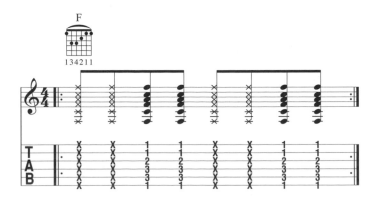

Track 21
00:12

Again, make sure your fretting hand is working together with your picking hand. You need to fret the chords when they're supposed to sound, let enough pressure off the strings for the scratch rhythms, and then quickly press down again for the chord hits.

Now let's try shifting *every* eighth note!

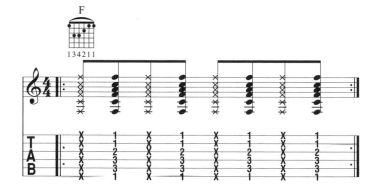

Track 21
00:19

This can get tricky for your fretting hand, which has to constantly move between fretting and damping. Slow things down if you have problems and then work it back up to speed. If this rhythm sounds familiar to you, it's because a whole genre of music uses this pattern as its foundation: Ska! The only difference is that ska players often use just the top strings, like this:

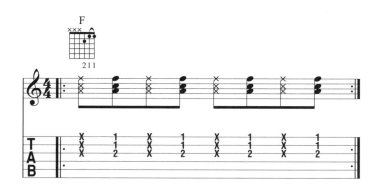

Track 21
00:27

TIP: WHAT'S THAT BELL-LIKE SOUND?

When you're playing scratch rhythm, you may occasionally hear some high-pitched bell-like tones coming from your guitar. If this happens, you're likely playing *harmonics* without intending to. Harmonics sound when you lightly touch a few specific spots on the guitar with one finger, but if more than one place on a string is touched, the harmonic won't sound. This usually means that if you're hearing harmonics, you're not using enough fret-hand fingers to dampen the strings, or perhaps not enough fingers are making contact with the strings. Make sure you have multiple fingers touching the strings and, if you still have problems, try sliding your fret-hand fingers just a little bit on the string in either direction until the harmonics stop. If you'd like to learn more about harmonics and how to play them, see **Chapter 10: Rhythm Fills**.

SCRATCH RHYTHM RIFFS

Scratch rhythms give more energy to some riffs because they keep the rhythm moving forward between chords. For instance, check out this simple riff on its own:

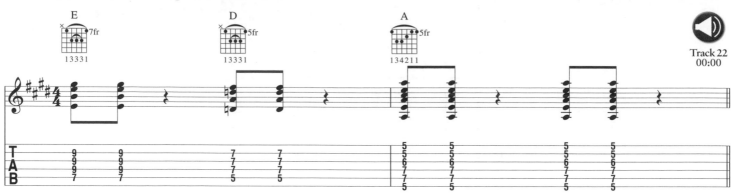

Add some scratch rhythm between chords, and the riff really comes to life. This one now sounds a little like the classic riff in Boston's "Long Time":

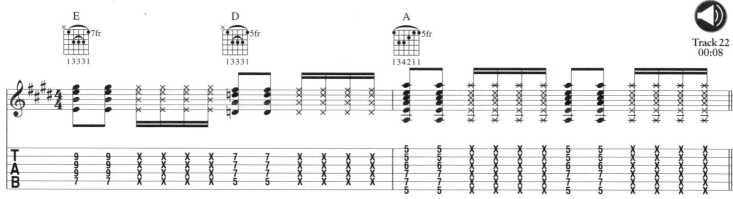

Let's try another one. This time, we'll look at the "Bo Diddley" beat that we learned back in **Chapter 5**:

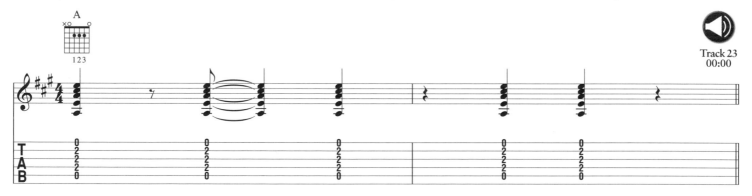

Adding scratch rhythm between this beat makes the riff much funkier:

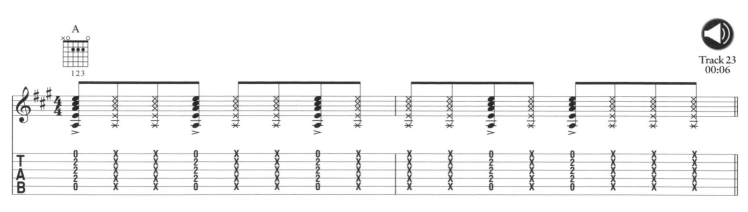

You'll find this kind of riff-driving scratch rhythm in a lot of funk music, and you can make almost *any* riff a little funkier with a bit of scratch rhythm. (See the "Single-Note Scratch Rhythm" gray box for a funky example.)

SINGLE-NOTE SCRATCH RHYTHM

Because of its rhythmic drive, many people choose to spice up their single-note riffs with scratch rhythm, too. We're working on our rhythm playing in this section, but don't forget about scratch rhythms when you're playing lead, because it can add that same funky groove to your lead riffs. Here's one example of a funky single-note riff that uses scratch rhythm:

Track 24
00:00

SCRATCH RHYTHM ON THE BACKBEATS

One great way to drive any song is to use an enhanced scratch rhythm on the *backbeats*. The "backbeats" are the second strongest set of beats in a regular measure—beats 2 and 4. If you listen to a drummer, you'll notice they usually hit the bass drum on the strongest beats (beats 1 and 3) and the snare on the backbeats (beats 2 and 4). Using scratch rhythm on the backbeats approximates the sound of the snare and gives your strumming that same extra pop that a snare does.

This type of scratch rhythm gets the most propulsion when you dig in a little harder. Dampen the strings with your fretting hand as you normally would, but also slap your picking hand into the strings so that your pick and the heel of your hand creates a crispier snapping sound than the typical "chukka chukka" of a normal scratch rhythm:

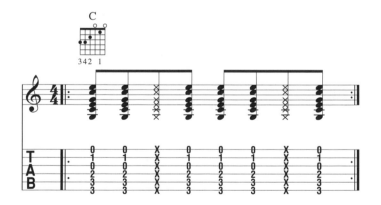

Track 24
00:16

Notice how I'm using a slightly different C chord here, with the added G note on the sixth string. I like the fuller sound of this C chord when I'm strumming scratch rhythm, but you can play a regular C chord if you have trouble with this four-fingered chord.

Using this strumming pattern can supercharge most any song with a similar strum pattern, and you can create countless strumming patterns around scratch rhythms on the offbeats. Here's an example that uses sixteenth notes and a chord change mid-measure that's used as a foundation in at least one of Jack Johnson's hits:

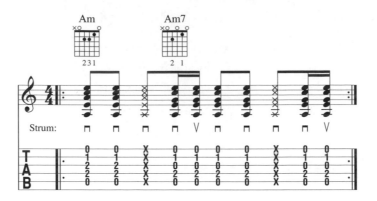

Track 24
00:24

Now let's try playing a song with scratch rhythms on the backbeats. "Midnight Special" is a classic tune recorded by countless acts over the years, including Leadbelly, Creedence Clearwater Revival, and Van Morrison.

> TIP: PICKUP MEASURE
>
> If you look closely at the first measure of "Midnight Special," you'll notice it only has three beats in it, while every other measure has four beats! When you have fewer beats than normal in the first measure, it's called a *pickup* measure, and the next measure is actually called the "first measure" of the song.

MIDNIGHT SPECIAL

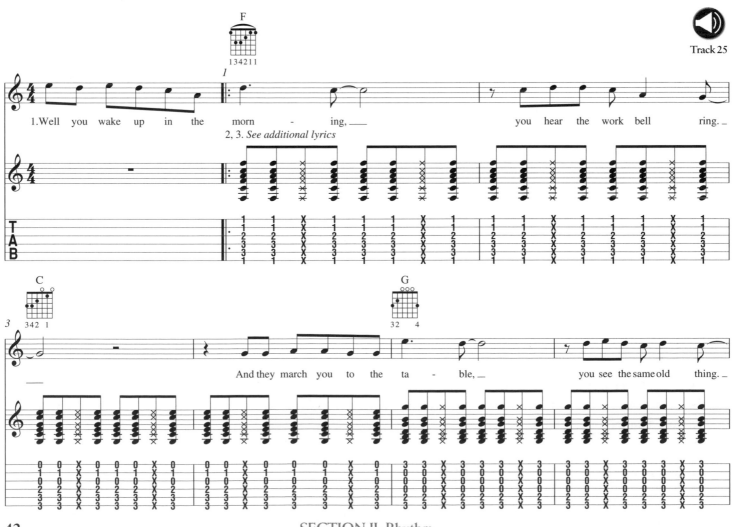

Track 25

SECTION II: Rhythm

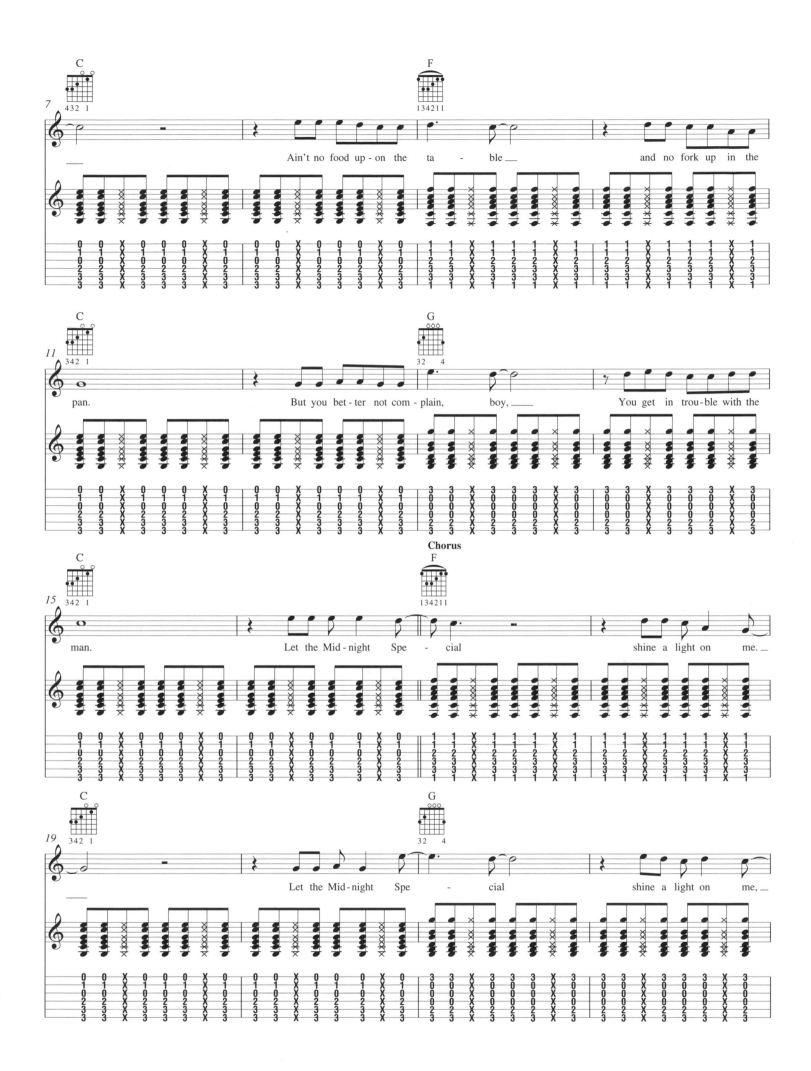

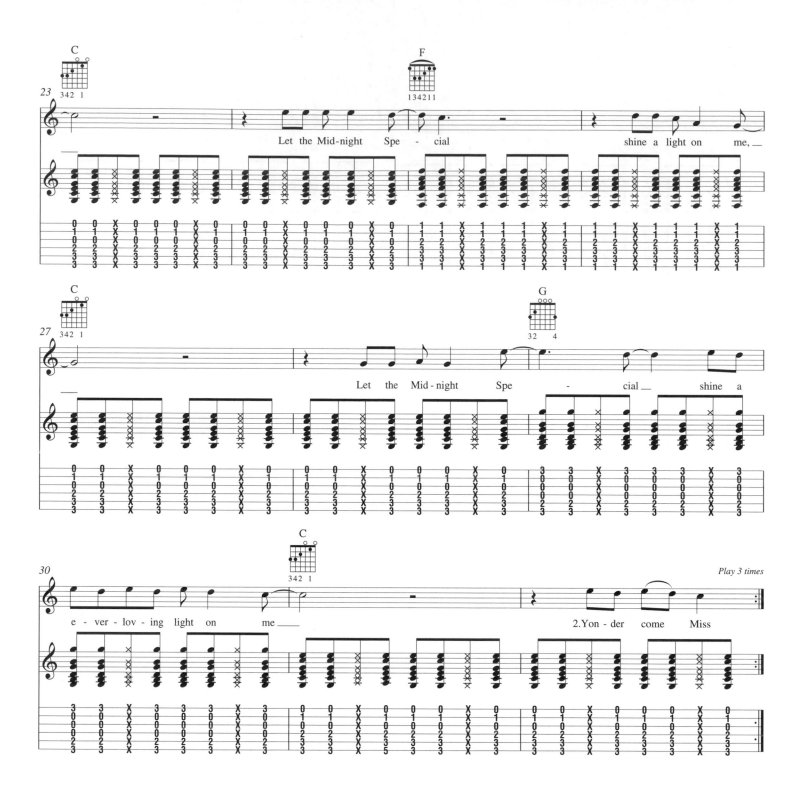

Additional Lyrics

2. Yonder come Miss Rosie, how in the world did you know.
   By the way she wears her apron and the clothes she wore.
   Umbrella on her shoulder, piece of paper in her hand.
   She come to see the gov'nor, she wants to free her man.

3. If you're ever in Houston, well, then you better do right.
   You'd better not gamble and you'd better not fight.
   Or the sheriff will grab you, and the boys will bring you down.
   And you can bet your bottom dollar, you're potentially bound.

SONGS WITH SCRATCH RHYTHM

• "Long Time"—Boston

• "Sitting, Waiting, Wishing"—Jack Johnson

• "Interstate Love Song"—Stone Temple Pilots

• "Night Moves"—Bob Seger

CHAPTER 8: OPEN-STRING CHORDS

You've probably noticed that the open strings on your guitar ring out far longer than any fretted note. This makes chords with a lot of open strings sound *huge*! Compare an open-position chord that uses open strings to a barred version of the same chord, and you'll see what I mean. So how can you harness that open-string effect when you're playing chords up the neck? Well, by adding open strings, of course! If you get creative with shapes, you can find some colorful sounding chords to bring into your songs.

In this chapter, the chord names may seem long or complicated, but don't worry too much about analyzing them if it makes you dizzy. (Of course, by all means dig deeper if you love theory! See the **Chord Theory** chapter in the appendix for more information on the chord names you'll find throughout this chapter.) The goal here is to show you some cool open-string shapes while also giving you the tools to experiment and find your own open-string chords. If the chord sounds good, then it works; if it doesn't, then move on to another shape or place on the neck.

SLIDE FAMILIAR SHAPES UP THE NECK TO BUILD OPEN-STRING CHORDS

You already know quite a few chord shapes, so a great way to start playing around with open-string chords is to experiment sliding those shapes up the neck to different places and seeing how they sound. Let's start with a D chord. Play a D chord and slide that shape around to see where it sounds good to you. Remember to still play just the top four strings when you slide the shape, just as you would a regular D chord. Here are some of the places I like:

D-SHAPE OPEN-STRING CHORDS

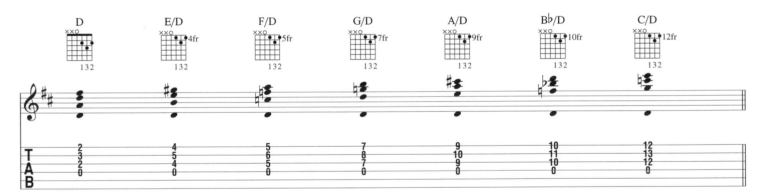

Before you know it, you already have enough chords to build a cool riff or intro progression. For instance, using these chords, we can come up with a progression that sounds a lot like the intro to the Beatles' "Eight Days a Week."

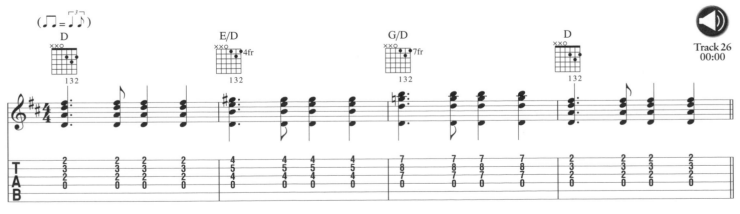

46   SECTION II: Rhythm

TIP: Slash Chords

If you're wondering about those chords with two letters separated by a slash, they're called *slash chords*. Slash chords are used when a different bass note is used for a chord; the chord name is first, and the bass note is listed after the slash. The "usual" bass note for any chord is called its *root*, and when a different chord tone from the root is in the bass, you say that the chord is in an *inversion*. But there are plenty of slash chords that have a bass note that isn't part of the chord at all. Either way, it's called a slash chord. In other words, all inversions are slash chords, but not all slash chords are inversions!

Now try the same thing with a C Chord. Here are the places I like this shape:

C-Shape Open-String Chords

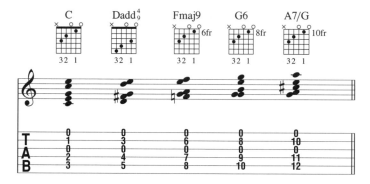

You can find this C shape used at the third fret in songs like Neil Young's "Sugar Mountain," which opens with a chord progression similar to this:

Neil Young-Type Progression

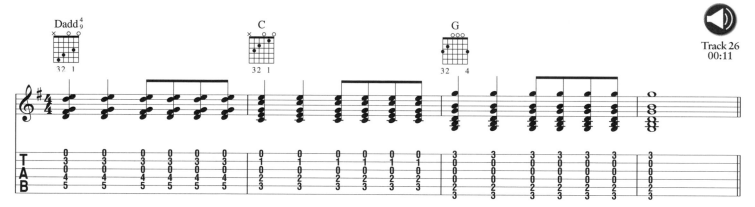

Track 26
00:11

Try experimenting with other shapes, as well. You can use smaller (or more obscure) shapes, or even partial chords or chord fragments. A Dm7 shape is a small shape, but it's also a partial shape—the top three strings of an F barre chord. Here's where I like this shape up the neck:

Dm7-Shape Open-String Chords

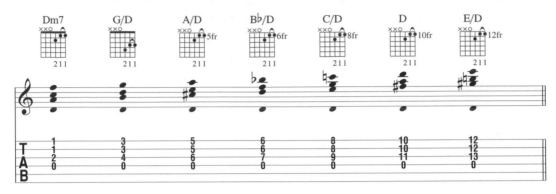

The fun happens when you mix shapes together to create unique progressions. But you can also use them as substitutes for more standard chords in a progression. For instance, instead of playing a D–G–A–G progression with standard chords at the nut, see how it gets a drone-like sound played with our Dm7 shape:

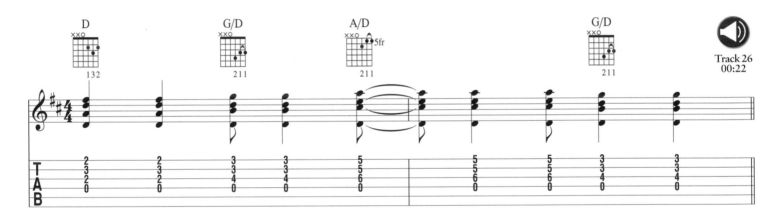

SLIDE MODIFIED BARRE SHAPES UP THE NECK FOR MORE OPEN-STRING CHORDS

E-SHAPE CHORDS WITH OPEN STRINGS

Barred shapes can also create some huge, lush-sounding chords. Here's how you create open-string chords with barre chords. Start with a barre-chord shape, like the F chord below:

SECTION II: Rhythm

Then, just leave out the barre, lifting your index finger to only play the bottom note, like this:

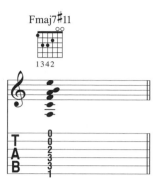

Fmaj7#11

Don't let that crazy name (F major seventh, sharp eleventh) intimidate you. You've probably already heard this chord before; flamenco guitarists frequently use a similar chord to alternate with an E chord:

FLAMENCO-TYPE PROGRESSION

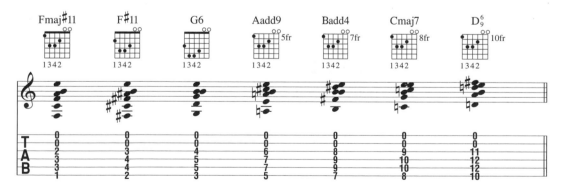

Track 26
00:29

Sliding this shape up the neck produces some huge six-string chords. Here are the ones I like:

E-SHAPE OPEN-STRING CHORDS

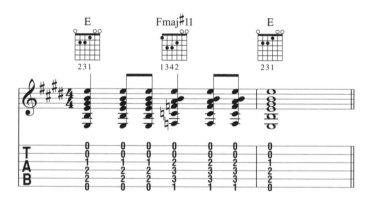

If you were playing a song in E that uses the "Wild Thing" progression, check out how these chords really fill out that E–A–B–A chord change:

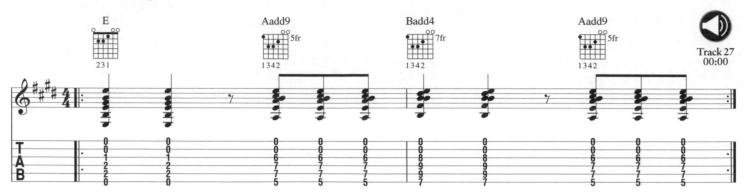

E7-SHAPE CHORDS WITH OPEN STRINGS

So far, we've been working with E-shape barre chords. Now let's try creating open string chords with another shape: the E7 shape. This time, let's play that E7 shape on the second fret (because it sounds a little discordant on the first fret!). If we leave the barre off again, that open fourth string sounds a little funky, so we'll leave a *partial barre* on strings 4–6, like this:

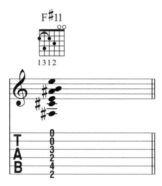

This shape feels a bit awkward, so we'll modify it a little bit more by leaving out the fifth string and switching our fingers around:

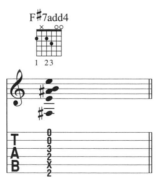

Here are the places I like this shape:

E7-SHAPE OPEN-STRING CHORDS

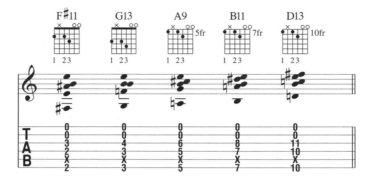

Pop one of these chords into an E–A–B progression, and it sounds more like "Twist and Shout" than "Wild Thing":

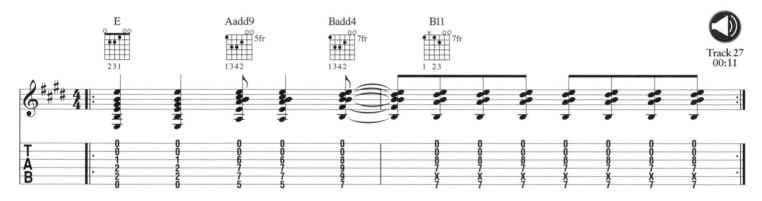

Track 27
00:11

EM-SHAPE CHORDS WITH OPEN STRINGS

Let's try one more E-based shape before moving on. This time, we'll look at an Em-shape barre chord. Let's try our Em-shape barre chord on the second fret. If we lift our barre here, that open third string sounds pretty terrible, so let's use our thumb to reach over the neck of the guitar and fret the sixth string, leaving our fingers free to fret the other notes. If this is uncomfortable for you, try a further modified shape, like the one on the below:

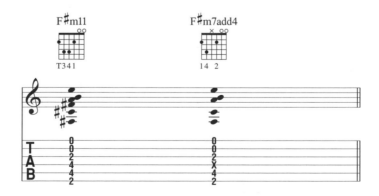

Here are the spots I like this Em shape:

EM-SHAPE OPEN-STRING CHORDS

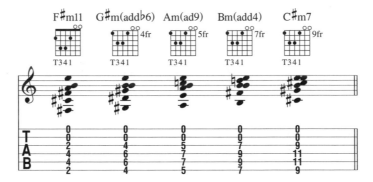

Another trick you can try with any barre-chord shape is to leave the bass note off, as well. The following example shows this in a progression that's similar to how the Allman Brothers' classic "Melissa" opens:

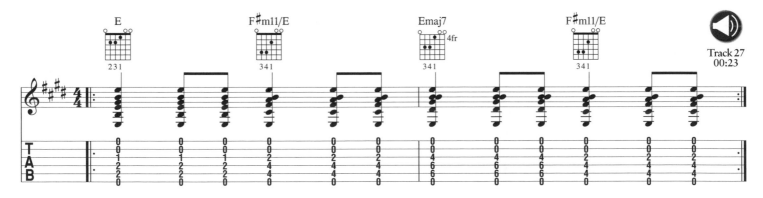

Track 27
00:23

A-SHAPE CHORDS WITH OPEN STRINGS

Now let's move up to A-shape chords. If we play an A-shape barre chord on the second fret and remove the barre, we get this:

That shape's pretty difficult to grab, so before you bust your fingers on it for too long, let's modify it a little by taking our fingers off of the second string and letting that open second string ring:

Here are the places on the fretboard where I like this shape:

A-SHAPE OPEN-STRING CHORDS

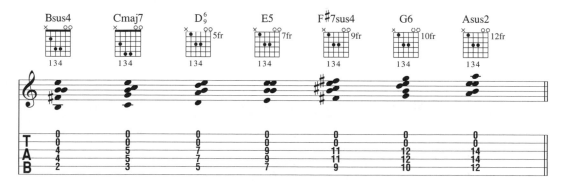

Now it's your turn! Try these shapes in your own songs and come up with more on your own. I've started you off using A-shape chords, so you can find your own A7-, Am-, or even Am7-shape chords. Then experiment with other shapes we haven't covered in this lesson.

To finish things off, let's try using some of these chords in a song—the timeless tune "Amazing Grace." The following version of the tune uses shapes from this lesson, but I've thrown in a few extra ones. Those first Aadd9 and Badd4 chords are just the top four strings of the E-shape chords we learned (which also show up in the song). I use these smaller shapes for a lighter sound in the first half of the verse. Notice how I've added a low open E string to the E5 chord in measure 9. Since it's already an E chord, that low string works fine as an addition and fattens up the low end quite a bit for the thicker-sounding second half of the verse. The E7 and B7sus4 chords in measures 10 and 14 are both modified A7 chord shapes slid up the fretboard, with the second and first strings left open. And that E chord in measure 12 comes from a C-shape chord, though slightly different from the ones we've seen earlier in the lesson. This one frets the third string note and leaves the first and second strings open.

AMAZING GRACE

Track 28

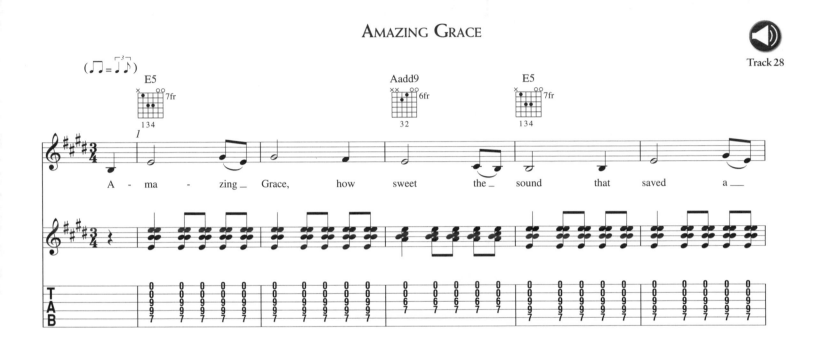

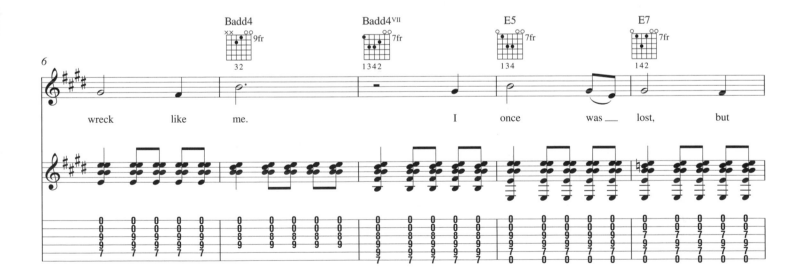

SECTION II: Rhythm

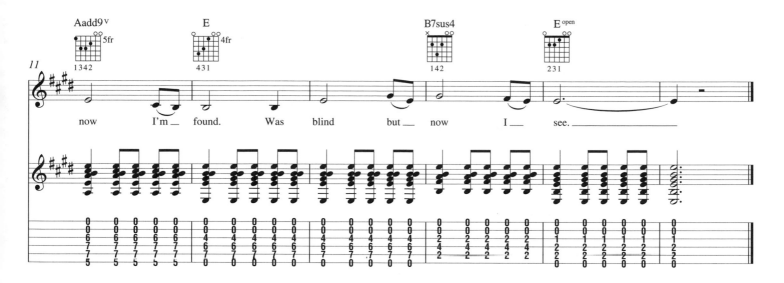

Words by John Newton
From *A Collection of Sacred Ballads*
Traditional American Melody
From Carrell and Clayton's *Virginia Harmony*
Arranged by Edwin O. Excell
Copyright © 2010 by HAL LEONARD CORPORATION
International Copyright Secured   All Rights Reserved

SONGS WITH OPEN-STRING CHORDS

- "Melissa"–The Allman Brothers Band

- "Daughters"–John Mayer

- "Sugar Mountain"–Neil Young

- "Closer to Fine"–Indigo Girls

CHAPTER 9: ARPEGGIOS

If chords are the "Clark Kent" in a guitar player's arsenal, then *arpeggios* are the "Superman" that guitarists pull out of their phone booth to transform those chords into more colorful sounds. Technically, you're playing an *arpeggio* when you play the notes of a chord individually. If you play the following example, you're already playing a C arpeggio:

Track 29
00:00

You can arpeggiate any chord, and you can also play your arpeggio in either direction:

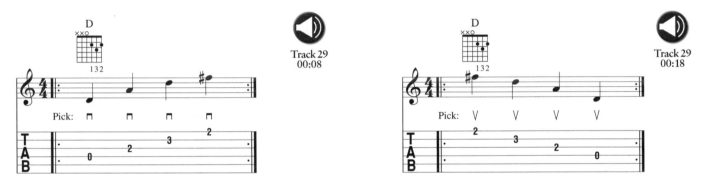

Track 29
00:08

Track 29
00:18

Notice the picking directions in the previous D-arpeggio examples. For an ascending arpeggio, try all downstrokes, as shown. For the descending arpeggio, try all upstrokes. This type of picking, called **economy picking**, uses the momentum of the pick to continue picking in the same direction whenever possible. Some guitarists prefer to play arpeggios and lead lines by always alternating down- and upstrokes (called **alternate picking**). I'll use economy picking throughout this chapter, but if you're not comfortable picking this way, try alternate picking instead. Of course, neither way may feel that easy at first! Whichever way you choose to play these examples, you should eventually get comfortable with both methods.

> **TIP: ALTERNATE PICKING VS. ECONOMY PICKING**
>
> *Alternate picking* uses alternating downstrokes and upstrokes, while *economy picking* uses the pick direction that takes the least amount of motion at any given time. Since alternate picking steadily alternates between strokes, it's much easier to keep your picking locked into a solid rhythm. Since economy picking economizes the motion in your picking hand, it allows you to play some things faster than you could with alternate picking. While both methods have their strengths, it's a good idea to get comfortable with both types of picking to bring your guitar playing to a higher level.

As you can see, a D-chord arpeggio perfectly fills out a measure when you play quarter notes. But what happens when you move to another chord that doesn't have four notes in it? One thing you can do is double back the other direction, as we do in the following C chord, which fills out two measures:

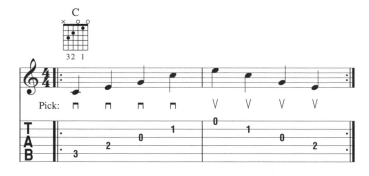

There are plenty of tricks you can use to make an arpeggio work for any song. For instance, if you're trying this same concept with a G chord and don't want the pattern to fill a gazillion measures, you can go up the arpeggio, turn the other direction, and then double back again, like this:

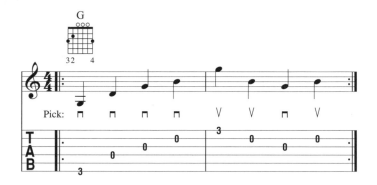

Notice that I skipped the A string in the last example. There aren't any set of rules you need to follow. People often think of arpeggios as always ascending or descending through the notes of a chord in order, but when we arpeggiate chords, we can pick notes out of the chord in any order we want. You can skip strings, change directions, and mix it up as much as you want to. Here's one way you can arpeggiate a D chord that sounds much different from our previous examples:

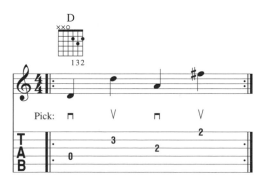

Or, you could play it like this:

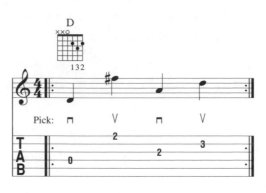

Track 30
00:22

You can also play arpeggios using eighth notes or sixteenth notes. Here are two examples using the previous arpeggio with eighth notes and sixteenth notes, respectively. As you can see, the pattern cycles through twice with eighth notes and four times with sixteenth notes.

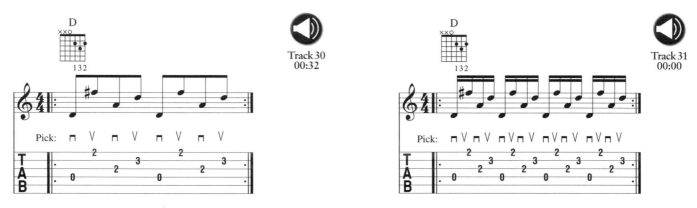

Now try playing the previous patterns we've looked at using eighth notes and sixteenth notes.

CREATING RIFFS WITH ARPEGGIOS

Now that you can play arpeggios, you don't need to do anything fancy to create cool arpeggio riffs with them: arpeggiating a few well-chosen chords starts to sound like a riff all by itself. The next example—which is similar to Green Day's "Good Riddance (Time of Your Life)"—transfers an arpeggio pattern from chord to chord to create an interesting riff-like sound that works well on its own or for backing up a singer.

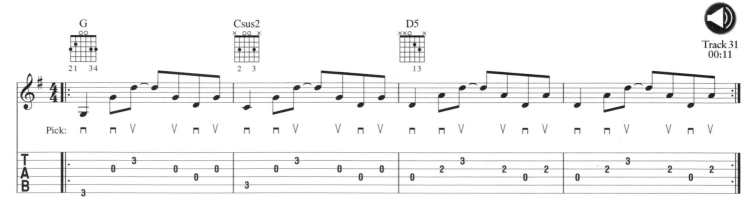

SECTION II: Rhythm

Arpeggio rhythm patterns like these have created some of the most classic riffs of all time, like the following example which is similar to Lynyrd Skynyrd's "Sweet Home Alabama." Check out how the first note in the pattern is repeated. You don't have to use arpeggios *all the time* to create a nifty arpeggio riff.

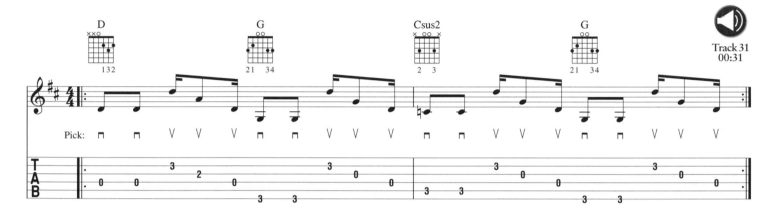

You can also create arpeggio riffs by sticking to the same chord but embellishing that chord by adding an extra note or two. In the following riff, I've used a common D-chord move that uses sus chords to create a riff:

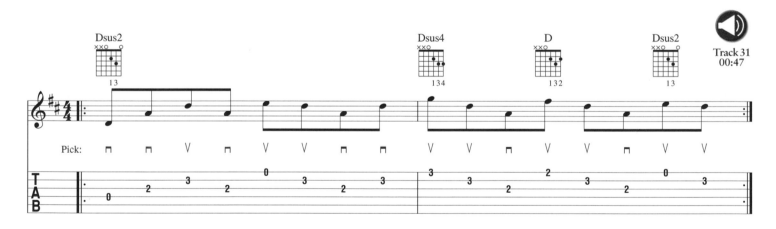

At this point, we've progressed fairly quickly through some pretty difficult arpeggios. Take your time to work through them all, apply these ideas to your own songs, and come up with your own arpeggio patterns.

To finish things off, let's ratchet the difficulty level back and use simpler arpeggios to play a complete song. We'll revisit "House of the Rising Sun" from the power chord lesson (in **Chapter 6**) because this song is often played this way. Here, though, we'll play standard root-position chords. Notice how the arpeggio pattern in the song transfers from chord to chord, changing only slightly to skip strings on some chords so that the up-and-down pattern sounds similar throughout.

HOUSE OF THE RISING SUN

Track 32

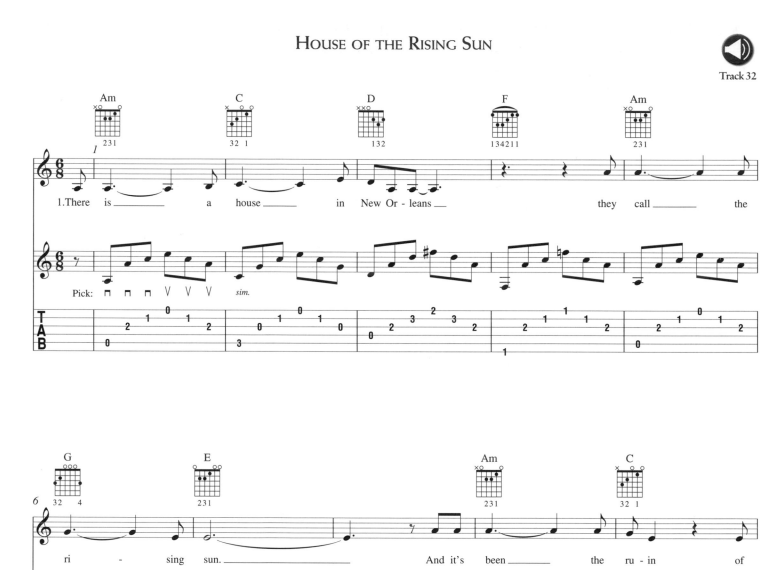

SONGS WITH ARPEGGIOS

- "Babe I'm Gonna Leave You"–Led Zeppelin

- "Sweet Home Alabama"–Lynyrd Skynyrd

- "Good Riddance (Time of Your Life)"–Green Day

- "Behind Blue Eyes" (intro and verses)–The Who

CHAPTER 10: RHYTHM FILLS

Strumming the same patterns without a break can make a song sound boring and predictable. The cure for this common illness is a small dose of *rhythm fills*. These are simply little breaks from the underlying pattern. They can drive a song forward, highlight a measure, or make the underlying strum pattern sound interesting again just by providing a short breather. Any instrument can play a fill, whether it's the drummer slapping the toms at the end of a chorus or the bass player swooping quickly up and down the neck before he enters a song. As a rhythm guitarist, we'll call our fills "rhythm fills."

It's important to remember that rhythm fills should be approached *conservatively*. As a rhythm player, your job is to hold down the rhythm first and foremost, and too many flashy fills can make a song disjointed and take away from the vocal or lead part.

LESS IS MORE

You don't have to do much to play a fill. In fact, any deviation from your strum pattern could be considered a fill. Say you're strumming all eighth notes in the key of C, like this:

Track 33
00:00

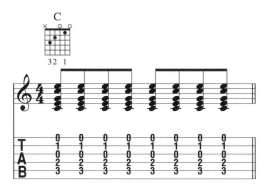

Now simply leave out a strum, and you have a fill!

Track 33
00:06

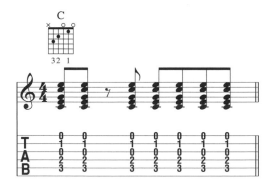

This may not sound like much, but let's put it in context, and you'll see what I mean. We'll put it at the end of a four-measure chord progression to see how it stands out:

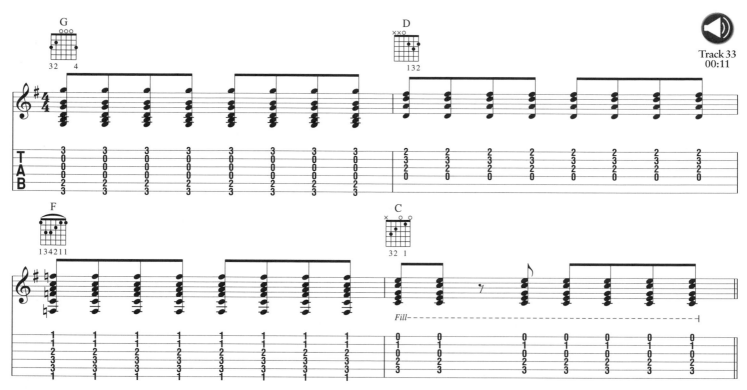

Anything can be a rhythm fill. To prove that point, I'll take the eighth-note strum pattern from our previous examples and make *that* a rhythm fill!

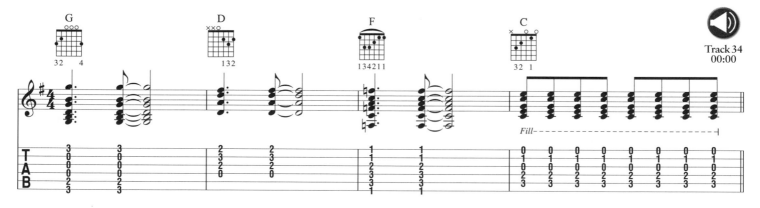

The most common way to create a rhythm fill is to change up the rhythm, and an easy way to do that is by adding accents. The next fill has an accented fill similar to what the Beatles play in their version of "Twist and Shout."

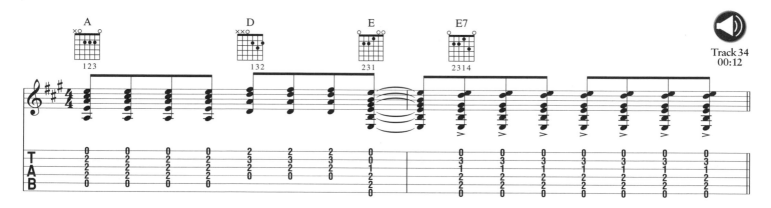

John Lennon's often cited as an underappreciated rhythm guitarist, and his rhythmic guitar fills are part of what made him a great player. Here's another simple example of how choppy accents can act as a great fill; this one's similar to Lennon's backup in "Norwegian Wood."

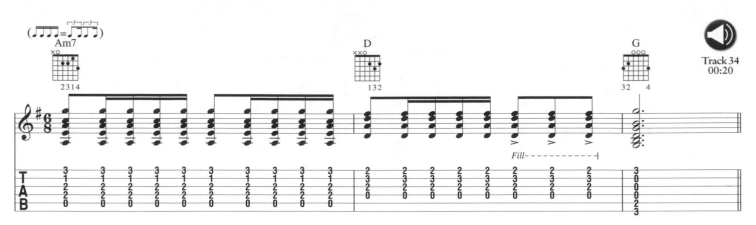

Sometimes a strum pattern already uses accents to highlight an internal rhythm. You can create an easy rhythm fill by eliminating all the unaccented strums and really digging in on the accented notes, like this:

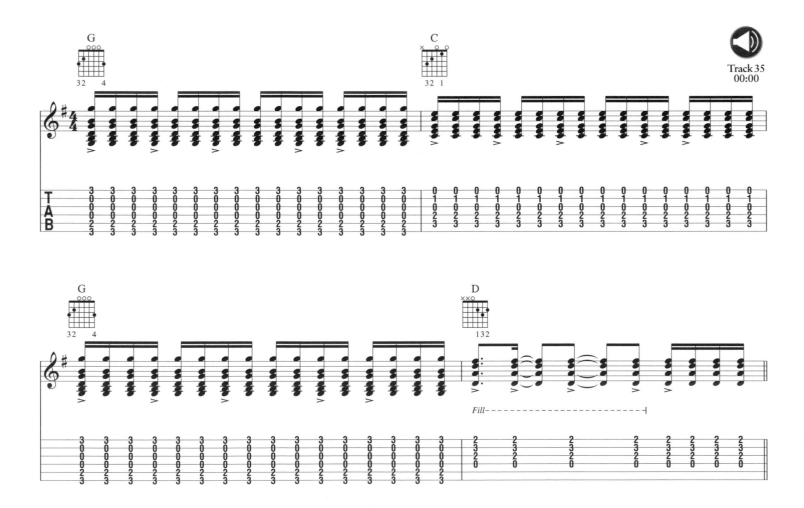

SECTION II: Rhythm

CHORDAL FILLS

Another way you can create rhythm fills is by inserting an extra chord or two into your rhythm pattern as a fill. To see how this works, let's look at a progression without a fill—this one in E, for instance:

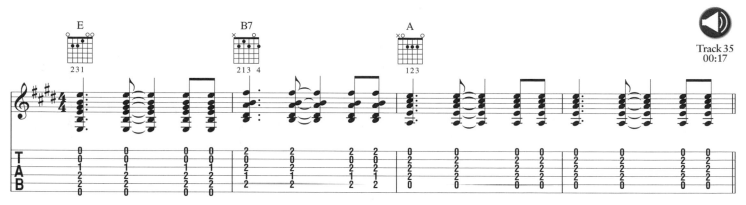

Now, let's add a quick fill by moving to D in the third measure.

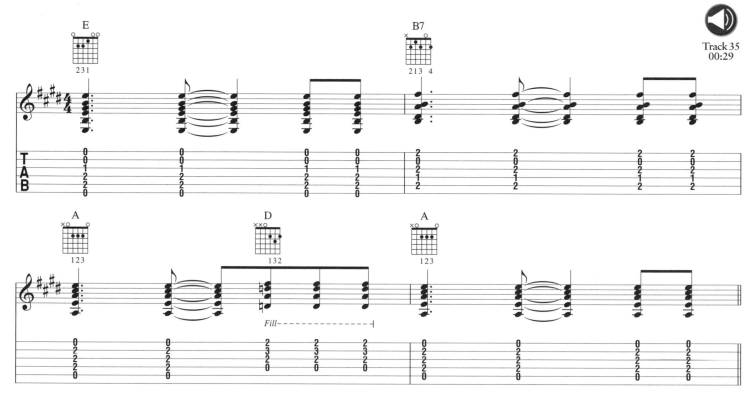

This type of fill sounds cool, and if you're playing by yourself, you can insert these kinds of fills whenever you want to. But if you're playing with other people, it's important to pay attention to how it fits with the other instruments. When you start changing the chords, things can start sounding awful mighty quickly! As long as you try your fill out with other instruments and it sounds good, then you're OK. (You can also tell the other players what you'll do and have them follow your fill.)

You can create less intrusive chordal fills by using partial chords for the fill, instead of full chords. Let's start with this C–D–G chord progression:

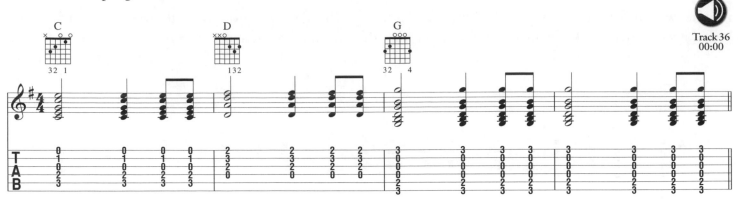

Now we'll add a chordal fill during the G chord by quickly touching on a C/G slash chord (a partial C chord, with a G in the bass. [See **Chapter 8** for more on *slash chords*.])

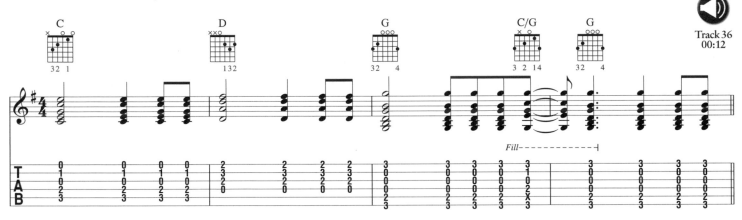

Pete Townshend used fills like this in many acoustic Who songs. Let's check out another favorite Pete Townshend-inspired fill at the end of a C–D–E chord progression. Here's the progression without the fill:

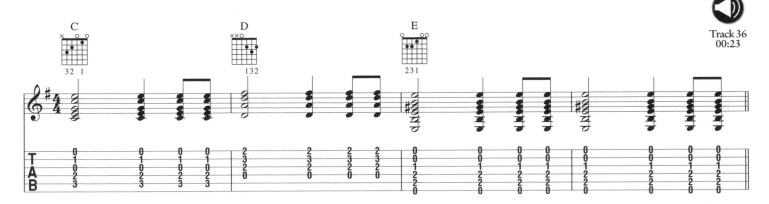

And here's the partial-chord fill inserted over the E chord:

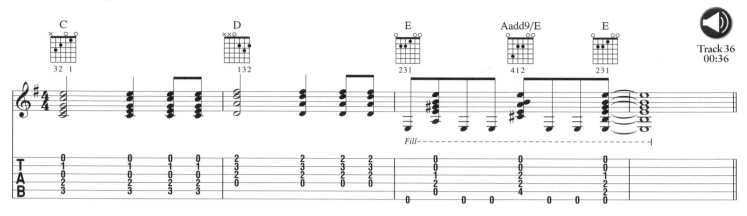

HARMONIC FILLS

You can also inject a different sound into your fills by playing a few harmonics (if you haven't played harmonics before, see the TIP sidebar on page 68). Here's a little fill that uses harmonics in a G–C–G chord progression:

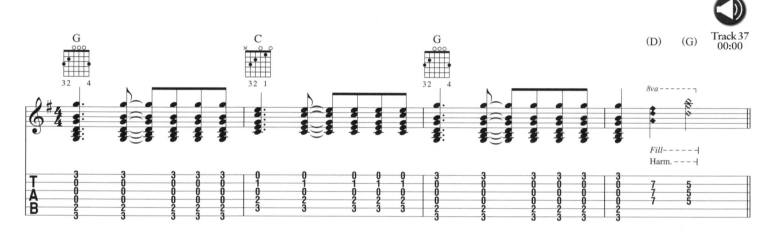

The harmonics in the previous example actually make up a D and G chord, respectively (I've placed those chord symbols in parentheses so you can see which is which). Since harmonics on strings 2–4 spell out the notes of a D or a G chord, they sound especially good in progressions in the key of D or G. But, harmonics don't have to fit the chord to make an interesting fill. Ani DiFranco, for instance, uses a ton of harmonic fills like the following one, where the harmonics don't relate as directly to the chord progression:

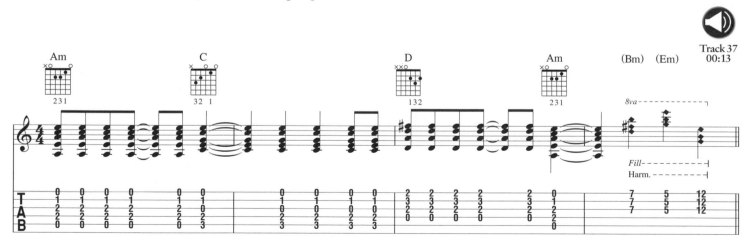

TIP: PLAYING HARMONICS

Harmonics are bell-like notes that sound when you touch a "node" on your guitar's string(s). When you strike a string, the vibration along the string looks like a wave; there are several places along the string where these waves "cross," and these places are called *nodes*. These nodes are where you can play harmonics. The most common places to play harmonics are at the fifth, seventh, and twelfth frets.

To play a harmonic, use your fret-hand finger to lightly touch the string *right above the fretwire* (not behind or between the frets). Don't press down on the string; simply touch it. Then, pluck the string or strings with your picking hand, and immediately lift your fret-hand finger off of the string. Before you try the multi-string harmonics found in this lesson, try some single-string harmonics, like this one on the twelfth fret of the high E string. Notice how the harmonic note has a diamond head and is labeled "Harm." between the notation and tablature staves:

Track 37
00:26

This is a fairly difficult technique, so don't be frustrated if the harmonic doesn't sound immediately. Coordinating the plucking with the lifting of your fret-hand finger can take a little practice to perfect. If you have trouble sounding the harmonic, work on this process, and make sure your fret-hand finger is directly over the fret.

Now let's insert a few rhythm fills into a song. We'll use "Man of Constant Sorrow," a staple of old-time and bluegrass circles. Check out how I've only used two rhythm fills in the whole tune—each one happening after the end of a vocal line (the first in measures 9–10 and the second in measures 19–20).

MAN OF CONSTANT SORROW

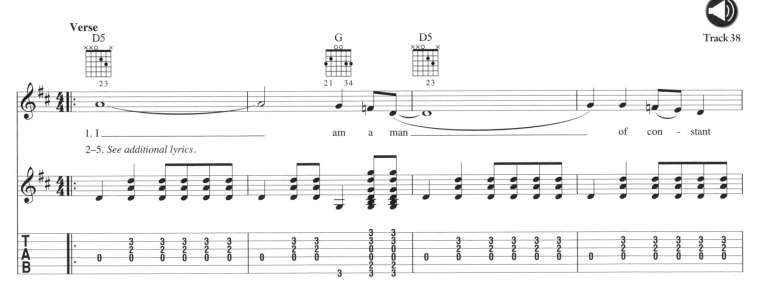

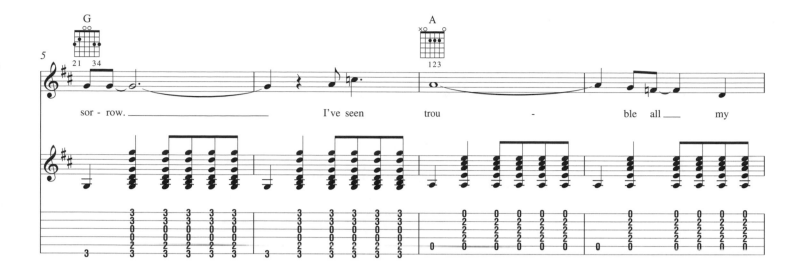

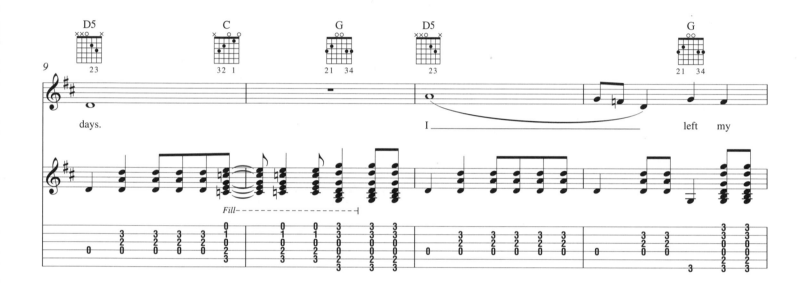

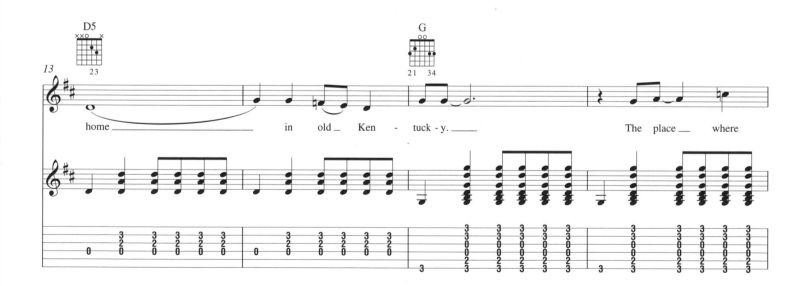

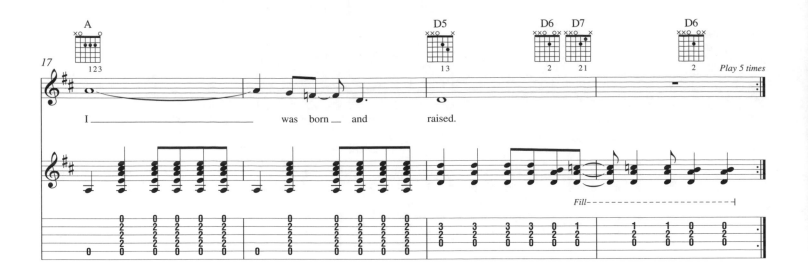

I _____ was born_ and raised.

Play 5 times

Fill - ⌐

Additional Lyrics

2. For six long years I've been in trouble.
   No pleasure here on earth I find.
   For in this world I'm bound to ramble.
   I have no friends to help me now.

3. It's fare thee well my own true lover.
   I never expect to see you again.
   For I'm bound to ride that northern railroad.
   Perhaps I'll die upon this train.

4. You can bury me in some deep valley.
   For many years where I may lay.
   Then you may learn to love another
   While I am sleeping in my grave.

5. Maybe your friends think I'm just a stranger.
   My face you never will see no more.
   But there is one promise that is given.
   I'll meet you on God's golden shore.

SONGS WITH RHYTHM FILLS

• "Big Yellow Taxi"–Joni Mitchell

• "Hey Hey What Can I Do"–Led Zeppelin

• "Out of Range (Acoustic)" (harmonic fills)–Ani DiFranco

SECTION III:
FINGERPICKING

In almost any musical genre, you'll find people picking their guitar's strings with their fingers instead of using a pick. Early blues singers, modern pop stars, new age guitarists, and folk singers through the ages have all used the technique. You'll even find a fingerpicker or two in bluegrass circles, where using a pick is so integral to the style that they call themselves "flatpickers!"

But fingerpicking is a stylistic choice. It's entirely possible you've learned to play with your fingers since day one because you chose to, but it's also highly likely that you've never played with your fingers before. If you're brand new to the technique, start with **Chapter 11: Easy Fingerpicking**. If you're already comfortable playing with your fingers, you might move quickly through it, but don't skip it completely; you might come across a technique or idea you haven't seen.

CHAPTER 11: EASY FINGERPICKING

In this chapter, we'll get comfortable using our fingers to pick the strings. Using each finger individually to pick the strings may seem difficult the first time you try it, but if you start with simple patterns, you'll get comfortable using each finger separately. There's plenty of time for the more complicated patterns later!

So, let's dive in and get started. First, place your thumb on the fourth string, and practice plucking that open string:

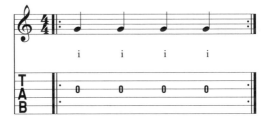

Track 39
00:00

That "p" between the tablature and notation staff means that you're playing the notes with your thumb (it actually stands for *pulgar*, a Spanish word meaning "thumb"). Along with "p" for "thumb," you'll see the following letters used to represent your other fingers: **i** = index finger, **m** = middle finger, and **a** = ring finger. Again, those letters stand for the Spanish names for each finger (*indice*, *medio*, and *anular*).

Now let's try your index finger on the open third string:

Track 39
00:09

Next, we'll move on to your middle finger on the open second string:

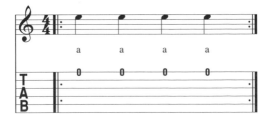

Track 39
00:18

We'll finish by playing the open first string with our ring finger:

Track 39
00:27

FIRST FINGERPICKING PATTERN

Now for the fun part! Let's put all those fingers together while playing a D chord. We'll keep the fingers on those same strings, start with the thumb and then pluck with each finger until we reach the ring finger. Repeat it until you're comfortable with the example.

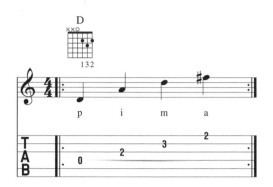

Track 40
00:00

Next, let's move to a C chord and try this same pattern. For this chord, we'll leave our fingers on the top three strings and move the thumb down one string to grab the bass note on the fifth string. In general, the thumb is responsible for any fngerpicked bass notes, so it roams the lower set of strings more than the other fingers.

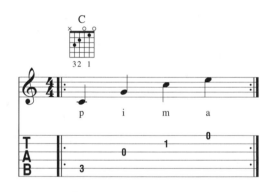

Track 40
00:10

You can transfer this exact pattern to any chord that uses those same five strings. Try out an A chord to see what I mean:

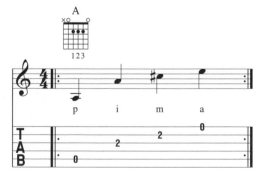

Track 40
00:21

Next, we'll try a G chord, which has its bass note way down on the sixth string. To play the same pattern we've been using, just slide that thumb down one more string to grab the bass note and leave those fingers on the top three strings.

Track 40
00:31

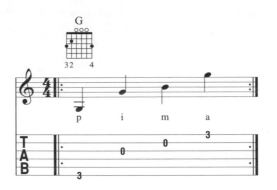

You can also play any six-string chords with this same pattern, like E, F, or Em. Try those out, if you like, before moving on. At this point, you're already playing a fingerpicking pattern that could work to back up many songs, but we're going to take it one step further before we finish this lesson.

> **TIP: NAILS, FINGERPICKS, ACRYLIC REINFORCEMENT, OR NOTHING?**
>
> There are plenty of options for your fingerpicking fingers, and each one affects the sound of your guitar and the way you play it. Some fingerpickers keep their nails trimmed short, plucking the strings with the fleshy part of their fingers. This gives the guitar a mellow tone. Other fingerpickers grow their nails out, plucking with a combination of flesh and nail, which produces a brighter and crisper sound. Many fingerpickers prefer this crisper sound, but keeping nails filed and healthy can be a high maintenance job. (Some people have thick, strong nails, while others have nails that break easily.) Players who want the sound of nails but have a difficult time keeping their nails from breaking might choose to get acrylic reinforcements; some may even go to a nail salon to have their nails done! For the brightest sound, there are a myriad number of plastic or metal fingerpicks and thumbpicks you can place over the tips of your fingers. Different fingerpicks work better for different motions (some are great for picking in a standard motion, but they hook the string when you try and pick backwards, flicking your finger in a frailing motion towards the floor). Thumbpicks require your thumb to strike at a completely different angle than without a thumbpick, although they're great for being able to switch back and forth between fingerpicking and flatpicking. No method of fingerpicking is better than any other. It's up to you to explore the options and decide which you like best.

UP-AND-BACK PATTERN

Let's extend our pattern to come back down after we've reached the highest note. We'll try this on a D chord first, and we'll shift to 3/4 time because the pattern works better here (and because our upcoming song is in 3/4 time).

Track 41
00:00

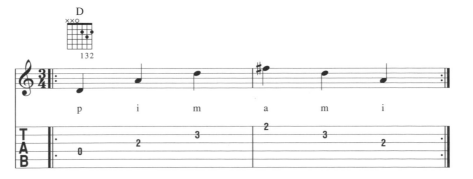

As you might guess, we'll try the same pattern with a five-string chord next. This time, instead of C or A, let's try Am for a little variety:

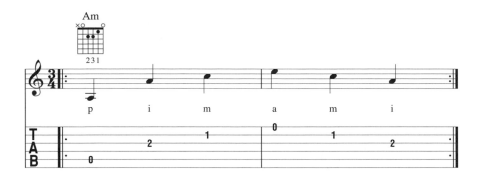

Track 41
00:11

To get familiar with this pattern on a six-string chord, let's try an Em:

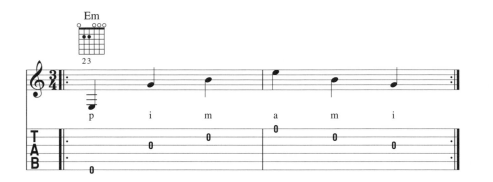

Track 41
00:22

At this point, you're ready to pick these patterns a bit faster. Let's run back through those last three examples using eighth notes for each one. If you trip over your fingers, slow things down, get comfortable, and gradually increase your speed until you're playing them as fast as they are on the track.

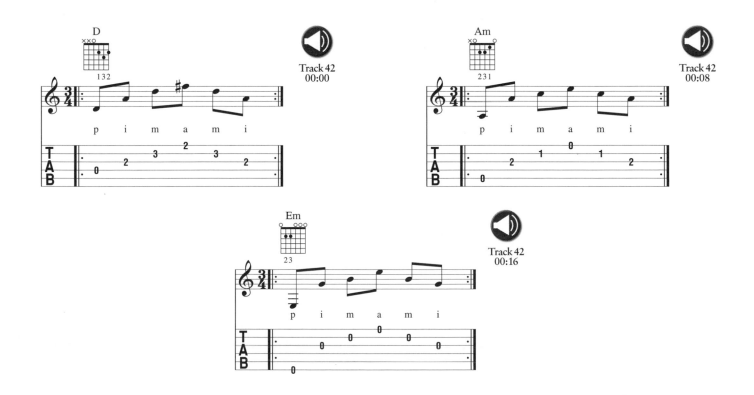

Now we're ready for a complete song! This version of the classic ballad "Scarborough Fair" uses our up-and-back pattern throughout the song. It's a good opportunity to practice changing chords while fingerpicking—especially on those relatively quick changes, such as in measures 6–9 and 18–21. If you have trouble switching quickly enough, you can start switching before the last eighth note of each measure. While your fret hand is moving to the next chord, you'll probably pluck an open string, but one open string between chords doesn't sound half bad and it's a common trick to cheat like this!

SCARBOROUGH FAIR

Track 43

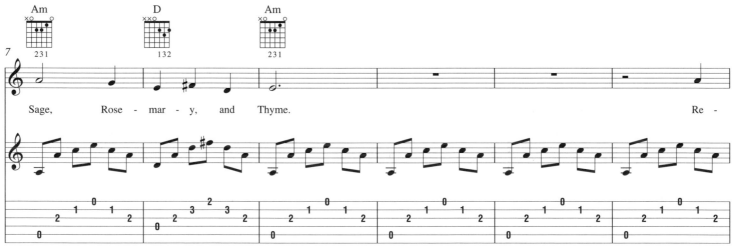

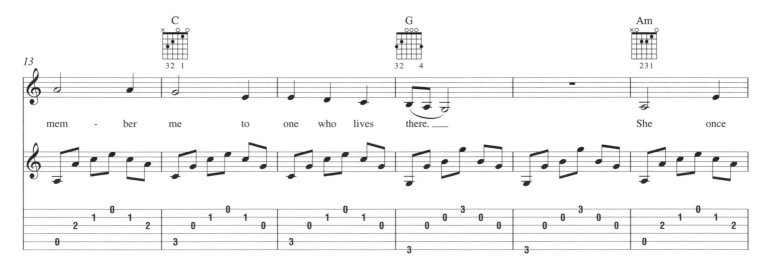

SECTION III: Fingerpicking

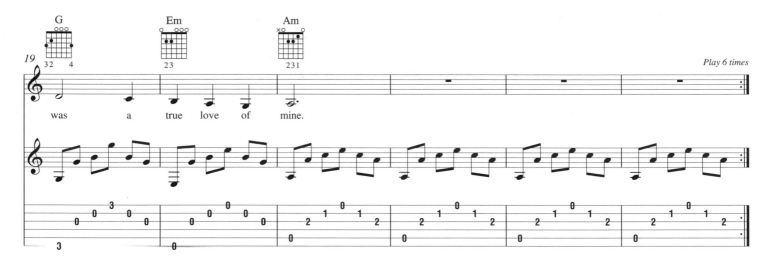

was   a   true   love   of   mine.

Additional Lyrics

2. Tell her to make me a cambric shirt.
   Parsley, Sage, Rosemary, and Thyme.
   Without any seam or needlework.
   Then she'll be a true love of mine.

3. Tell her to wash it in yonder dry well.
   Parsley, Sage, Rosemary, and Thyme.
   Where ne'er a drop of water fell.
   Then she'll be a true love of mine.

4. Tell her to find me an acre of land.
   Parsley, Sage, Rosemary, and Thyme.
   Between the salt water and the sea strand.
   Then she'll be a true love of mine.

5. Plow the land with the horn of a lamb.
   Parsley, Sage, Rosemary, and Thyme.
   Then sow some seeds from north of the dam.
   Then she'll be a true love of mine.

6. Tell her to reap it with a sickle of leather.
   Parsley, Sage, Rosemary, and Thyme.
   And gather it all in a bunch of heather.
   Then she'll be a true love of mine.

CHAPTER 11: Easy Fingerpicking

CHAPTER 12: ALTERNATE BASS FINGERPICKING

Alternate bass fingerpicking is one of the most common fingerpicking methods you'll hear. Country star, Merle Travis, used his version of it so much that it's often called "Travis picking," but you're as likely to hear this style of fingerpicking in a pop, folk, or alternative song as you are to hear it in a country tune.

So, what exactly *is* alternate bass fingerpicking? If you're fingerpicking, and your bass is alternating between notes, then you're playing alternate bass fingerpicking. So, to start, let's practice playing a bass note that alternates between notes. We'll start with a C chord and alternate with the thumb between the fifth and fourth strings, like this:

Track 44
00:00

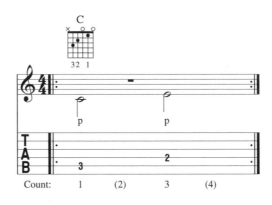

As your thumb thumps steadily along on the beats, try adding your middle finger on beat 2:

Track 44
00:07

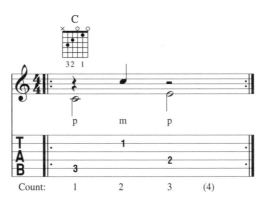

Finally, add in your index finger on beat 4, and you're playing an alternate bass fingerpicking pattern:

Track 44
00:15

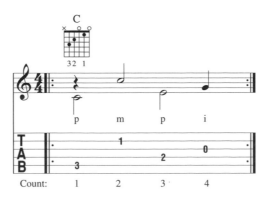

Congratulations! You're already playing an alternate bass fingerpicking pattern. Now, to bring this up to regular speed, we'll play it twice as fast, with your thumb striking on each beat, and your fingers playing on the offbeats:

Track 44
00:22

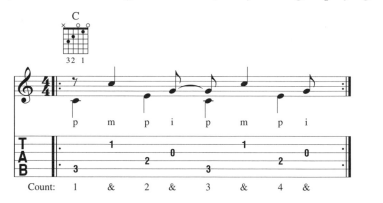

Don't get intimidated by the tied notes in the up-stemmed layer. Just remember that your fingers should play on every offbeat—every time you count "&" between each beat.

You can transfer this pattern to any chord with its bass on the fifth string: A, Am, B7, Bm, and any other chord you can think of, including barre chords. Let's test this out on an A chord:

Track 45
00:00

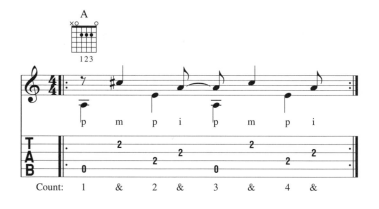

TIP: Two Layers of Notes with Split Stems

Up until this chapter, you've only seen notes in one layer. Notice how the examples in this chapter split the notes into two layers: one set has the stems going down and one set has the stems going up. Fingerpicked parts are often notated this way to make them easier to read. When this happens, the notes you play with your thumb usually have stems pointing down, while the notes you play with your fingers have stems pointing up.

To transfer our fingerpicking pattern to chords with their bass note on the sixth string, play everything exactly the same, except move your thumb down to the sixth string on beats 1 and 3 (instead of playing the fifth string). Here's that pattern on a G chord:

Track 45
00:08

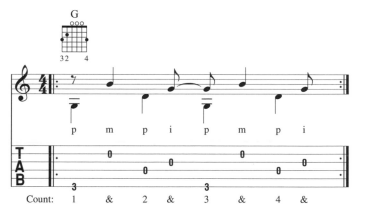

As you may have guessed, you can transfer this pattern to any chord with a bass note on the sixth string, like E, F, and others.

The last chord we'll look at is a D chord—one of the few chords with its bass on the fourth string. To play this pattern with a D chord, get your fingers in position to play a C chord pattern and move them all up one string (including your thumb) so that your index finger is now on the first string:

Track 45
00:16

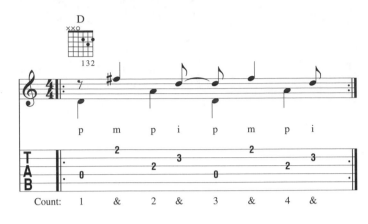

ADD THE RING FINGER FOR VARIETY

One way you can add variety to your alternating bass patterns is to occasionally use your ring finger instead of your middle finger. Let's try this out on a C chord to see how it works. We'll use our ring finger for the first upstemmed note—on the "&" of beat 1, and we'll use it to play the first string, like this:

Track 46
00:00

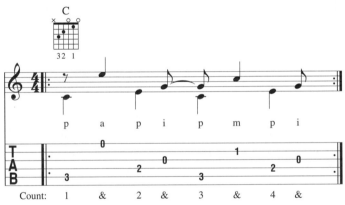

You can't transfer this pattern to the D chord because the ring finger wouldn't have a string to play beyond the first string! But, you can play this for chords that have a bass note on the sixth string, like the E chord:

Track 46
00:08

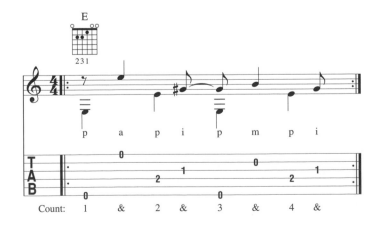

ADD A PINCH

You can also add variety by using a "pinch." A *pinch* happens when you play a note with a finger at the same time you play one with your thumb. When you do this, your middle-finger note shifts forward from the "&" of that beat to the beat itself, like this:

Track 46
00:16

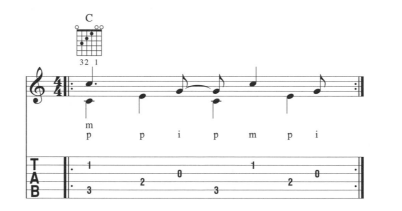

You can play a pinch with any bass note, though they're rarely played on every beat. Here's a pinch with your index finger. Notice how I've left out the middle finger immediately preceding this pinch, since it sounds a little awkward:

Track 46
00:25

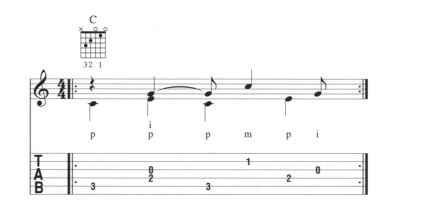

The possibilities are endless. As long as you keep that bass alternating with your thumb, you can do most anything you want to with your fingers.

MORE ALTERNATING IN THE BASS

You can also dress up your alternate bass picking patterns by alternating the lowest bass note with a different string. For an A chord, use the sixth string on beat 3 instead of the fifth string:

Track 47
00:00

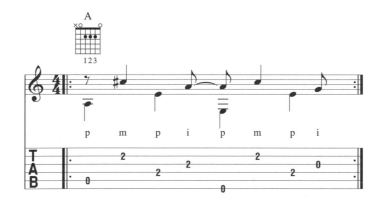

For an E chord, you can alternate the sixth string bass note with the fifth string on beat 3:

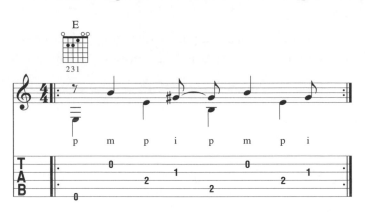

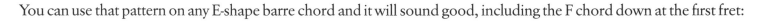

You can use that pattern on any E-shape barre chord and it will sound good, including the F chord down at the first fret:

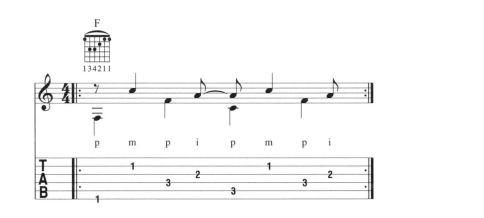

For a C chord, alternate the bass note with the third fret of the sixth string. To do this, you'll have to move your ring finger from the fifth string down to the sixth string in the middle of the measure and move it back up to the fifth string to play the next bass note. Make sure to keep the rest of your fingers planted on the C chord.

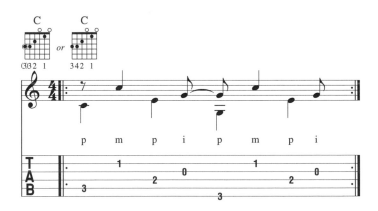

MIX IT UP

We've looked at quite a few difficult ideas in this lesson already, so don't worry if you haven't mastered it all quickly. Most pickers use only one or two of these ideas at once in a song, but your options open up a whole lot more when you come up with your own patterns by mixing these ideas together.

Here's one example of what you could do by adding a pinch at the beginning and leaving off the final note. Kerry Livgren used this pattern, along with a shifting chord progression, for "Dust in the Wind," one of Kansas' biggest songs.

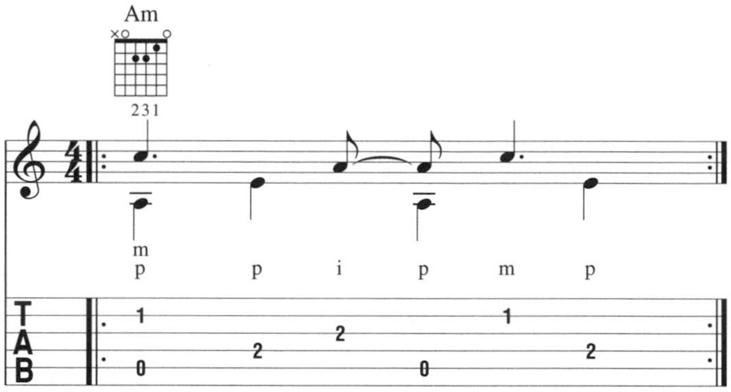

Track 48
00:00

John Lennon used a similar pattern, with the extra alternating bass, for the Beatles' song "Julia."

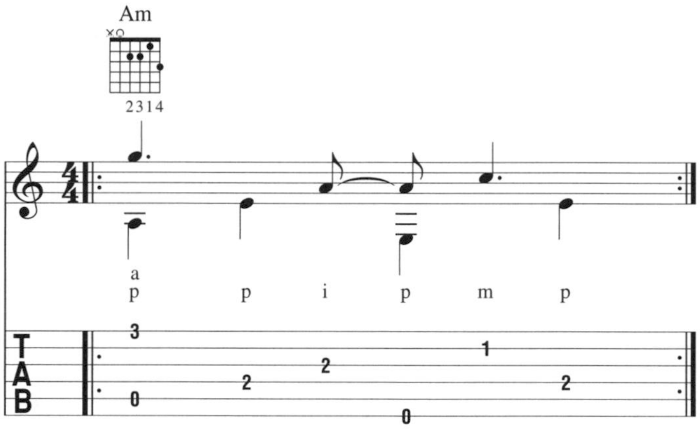

Track 48
00:08

Now let's try a few of these patterns in a song. The following version of "Frankie and Johnny" mostly uses our original pattern with the extra alternating bass throughout, with the exception of two pinches: one on an A chord in measure 4 and the other on the E chord in measure 9.

TIP: Triplet Feel

"Frankie and Johnny" is played with a *triplet feel*. Each pair of eighth notes has a long note followed by a short note—the first note is actually twice as long as the second note. An easy way to think about it is to visualize a measure of triplets (see the example on the left) with the first two triplets in each beat tied together. When a triplet feel is designated at the beginning of a song, it's written like the example on the right, but it's played like the example on the left.

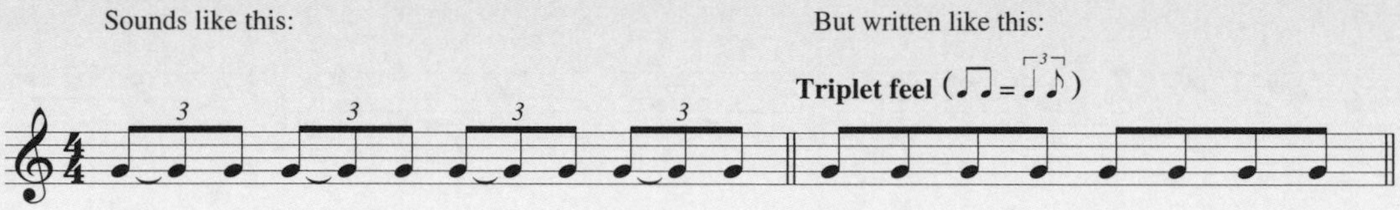

You'll also see triplet feels labeled as "shuffle feel" or "swing feel" (swing music uses the triplet feel so often that the "swing feel" is a triplet feel).

FRANKIE AND JOHNNY

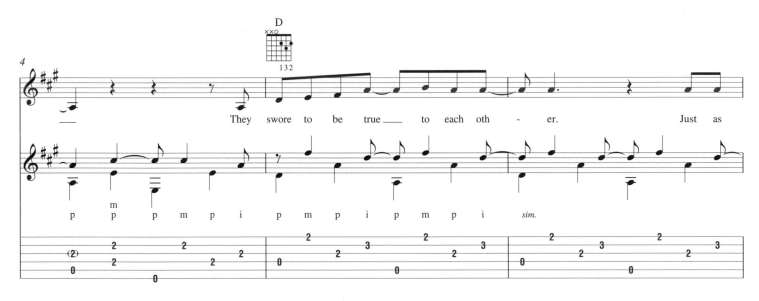

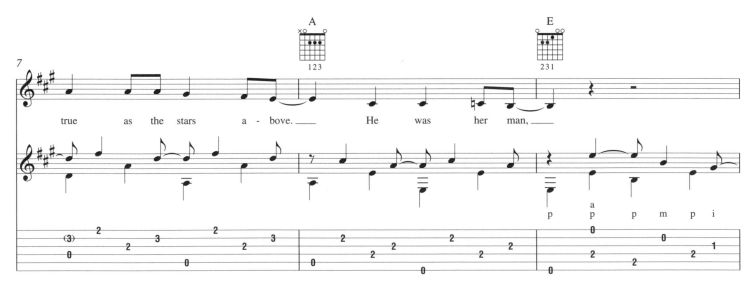

SECTION III: Fingerpicking

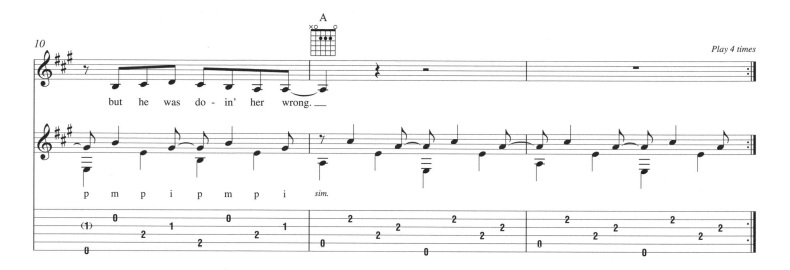

Additional Lyrics

2. Frankie went down to the corner
   To get a bucket of beer
   She said to the old bartender
   "Has my lovin' man been here?"
   He was her man, but he was doin' her wrong.

3. Frankie looked over the transom door
   To see what she could spy.
   There sat Johnny on the sofa
   Just lovin' up Nellie Bligh.
   He was her man, but he was doin' her wrong

4. Frankie got down from that high stool,
   Didn't want to see no more.
   Root, toot, toot, three times she did shoot
   Right through that hardwood door.
   He was her man, but he was doin' her wrong.

Songs with Alternate Bass Fingerpicking

• "The Boxer"–Simon & Garfunkel

• "Such Great Heights"–Iron & Wine

• "Julia," "Dear Prudence"–The Beatles

• "Lost Cause"–Beck

CHAPTER 13: MONOTONIC BASS FINGERPICKING

Monotonic bass fingerpicking is that static, thumping bass sound that solo acoustic blues players like Big Bill Broonzy used as a backdrop to their blues melodies and improvisations. More recent blues-influenced rockers like Led Zeppelin and Eric Clapton have kept this style alive in their acoustic sets, and it's continued to stay popular among roots and blues players to this day.

Unlike the alternate bass fingerpicking from **Chapter 12**, monotonic bass fingerpicking stays on the same bass note, like this:

Track 50
00:00

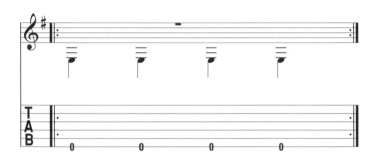

Since this bass is much easier to play than the alternating bass we played in the last chapter, you might rightfully wonder why in the heck we're doing this in a later chapter! Here's the answer: while the bass is simpler, the melody notes get much more complicated. Most alternate bass fingerpicking is used as a rhythmic accompaniment part, with the same patterns repeated over and over again. Monotonic bass, on the other hand, is often used underneath melodies and solos that are not based on repeated patterns. Guitarists using this technique often use it to play instrumental songs on their guitar that stand on their own without any vocals, though you *can* sing over this style as well, if you want to.

MELODIES OVER A THUMPING BASS

Since we'll be playing melodies over our steady bass notes, we need some method to create those melodies, and a good place to start is by using the minor pentatonic scale. The *minor pentatonic scale* is a five-note scale that most guitarists learn before any other scale. It's the foundation for almost all blues soloing and it also works great for pop and rock songs (for more on the minor pentatonic scale, see **Chapter 16: The Minor Pentatonic Scale**). In this lesson, since we'll be playing in the key of E, we'll draw our melodic ideas from the E minor pentatonic scale.

Track 50
00:08

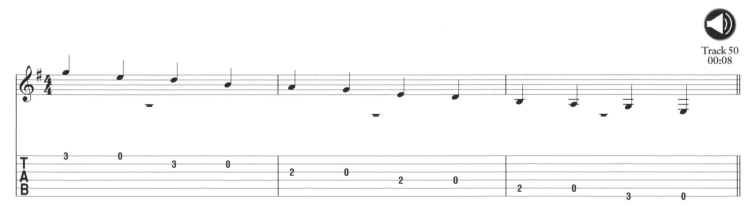

Once you have that form under your fingers, practice running it up and down over your low E bass note. Since we're playing that low bass note, we'll leave out the notes on that string from the scale:

Track 50
00:18

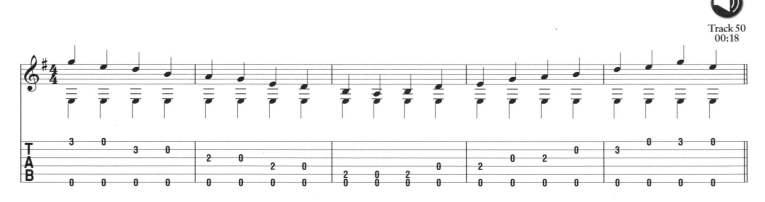

TIP: WHICH PICKING-HAND FINGERS SHOULD I USE?

Notice how there are no pick-hand fingerings given in this chapter. You'll want to use your thumb for all of the notes with stems pointing down. The interesting part is choosing which fingers to play the up-stemmed notes, and there are plenty of ways you can play each example. Without the recurring patterns of alternate bass fingerpicking, it's less important to play everything exactly the same way.

When you're playing passages that have one note per string, it's helpful to assign one finger to each string—for instance, your index, ring, and middle fingers on the third, second, and first strings, respectively. Then, when you have a melody note on the fourth string, you can move your index finger down one string to grab that, or even move all three fingers down one string to be ready for a whole set of notes on the second through fourth strings.

When playing two or more notes on the same string, some players (especially Classical guitarists) alternate with two fingers—usually their index and middle fingers; this allows you to play quicker melody lines.

As far as how many fingers you should use, it's a matter of preference. Some blues players use their thumb, index, and middle fingers, and others use only their thumb and index finger! But I encourage you to try using your index, middle, and ring fingers (and even the pinky when the need arises).

Play around with this scale a bit, and make sure to mix the rhythm up as well. Just running up and down the scale with quarter notes sound more like a scale than a melody. Here's a lick you can try to get you started:

Track 50
00:32

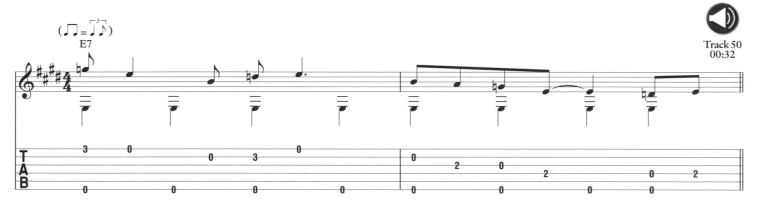

Blues songs in E use more than just an E7 chord. They also use A7, so practice that E-minor pentatonic scale over an A bass, as well. Note how there are fewer notes we can play over A, since the A bass note keeps us from using notes on the fifth string:

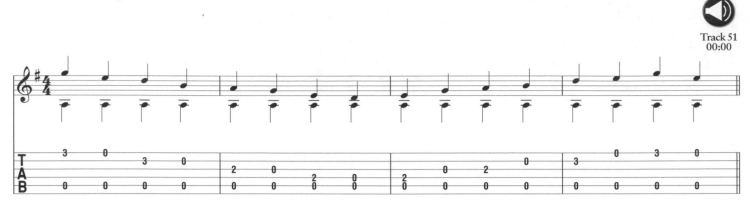

Track 51
00:00

You may also notice that it sounds a bit different when playing this scale over an A bass, but you can still come up with licks you like. Let's manipulate our E lick to make something similar over the A chord:

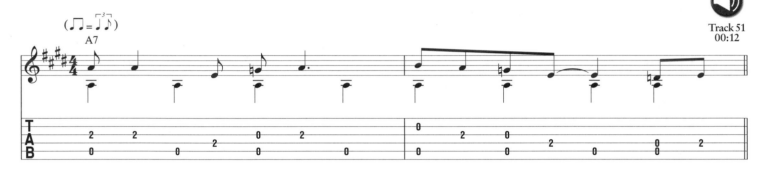

Track 51
00:12

Of course, context is everything, and practicing E minor pentatonic licks over an A bass by itself sounds different than those same licks over an A bass when it's in the middle of a blues progression in E. To see what I mean, here's the same lick we played over an E, but this time it's over the A. Notice how it sounds just a little off:

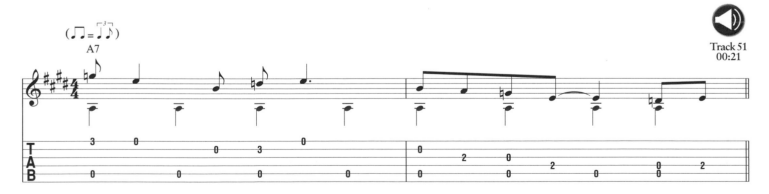

Track 51
00:21

Now let's hear the lick within the context of a blues progression. A standard blues progression is 12 measures long (and our final song is actually an extended 15 measures), but we'll just look at the first eight measures here, which are made up of four measure of E followed by two measures of A, and then two more measures of E.

Notice how this lick sounds much better in the context of the blues progression—something to keep in mind as you come up with your own licks and phrases.

The other chord in an E blues is a B7 chord. For the E7 and A7 chords, we have an open bass string handy which allows us to use all our fingers to play licks (it also allows us to freely move higher up the fretboard). Since you have to fret the B bass note of a B7 chord, you have much less freedom. Because of this, people often play more rhythmic or chordal sounds over the B chord in an E blues—something like this:

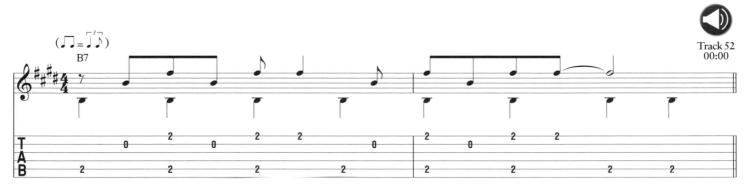

One trick people use to make the B7 section sound more interesting is to slide the chord up a half step to play a C7 chord and then slide it back down again. When you do this, make sure to dampen the open B string for that C7 chord (it doesn't sound too good).

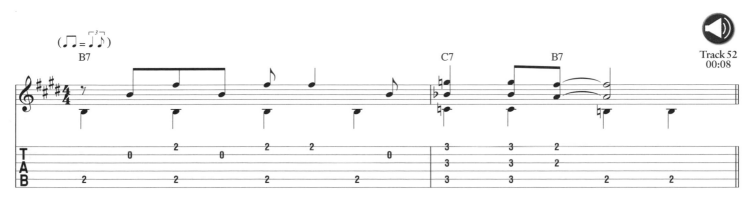

CHAPTER 13: Monotonic Bass Fingerpicking

LOW BASS BLUES

Now that we're comfortable playing our monotonic bass with the E7, A7, and B7 chords, let's put it all together and play a complete blues song. "Low Bass Blues" is based around a popular sliding blues lick at the third fret. Slide into the fourth fret of the third string with your middle finger and follow that up with your index finger on the third fret of the second string:

Track 52
00:16

There are so many ways you can use this lick. Here's one way that uses triplets and slides back down to open position on the last beat, which is another common addition to this lick:

Track 52
00:22

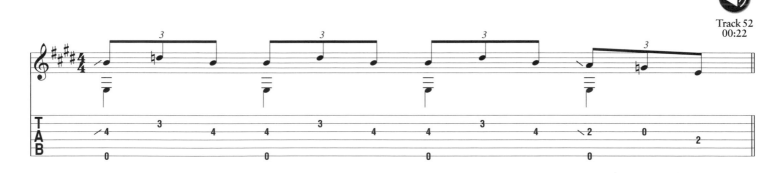

In "Low Bass Blues," we'll slide into this lick and leave our fingers on the fourth and third frets throughout the first one-and-a-half measures. To get that first measure to work, you'll have to lift your index finger off of the second string on beat 3, and then put it back at the start of measure 2, where you'll need to play the third fret. The open third string on the "&" of beat 2 in measure 2 gives you time to move your hand down to open position to grab the notes on the second fret. Then, you can bring your hand back up as you play the open strings in measure 3, letting it float above the frets until it's time to play those notes at the end of the measure.

Over the A7 chord, we're playing the exact same licks, with one exception—that second-fret C♯ note on beat 3 of measure 5. To grab this note, you'll need to quickly slide your index finger down from the third fret and then bring it back up to play the note on the third fret in the next measure. This is a bit tricky to play, but if you slow it down, you should be able to get the hang of it. Feel free to slide both your index and middle fingers down a fret, so that you don't have to stretch too much.

Notice how the bass line walks into a few of the chord changes. In measure 8, move up to the A string on beat 3, and move through the open string and first fret to reach the second-fret B note at the beginning of the next measure. In measure 10, you walk back through the first fret on beat 4 to reach the A bass note in the next measure.

The rest of the song doesn't throw too many tricks at you, except for the turnaround in measure 11. A *turnaround* is a figure used at the end of a progression to either wrap things up or lead things back to another repeat of the progression. Here, we're using a common trick that takes our two-note shape and slides it down one fret at a time until we reach the open position, at which point we finish with an E7 chord.

LOW BASS BLUES

Track 53

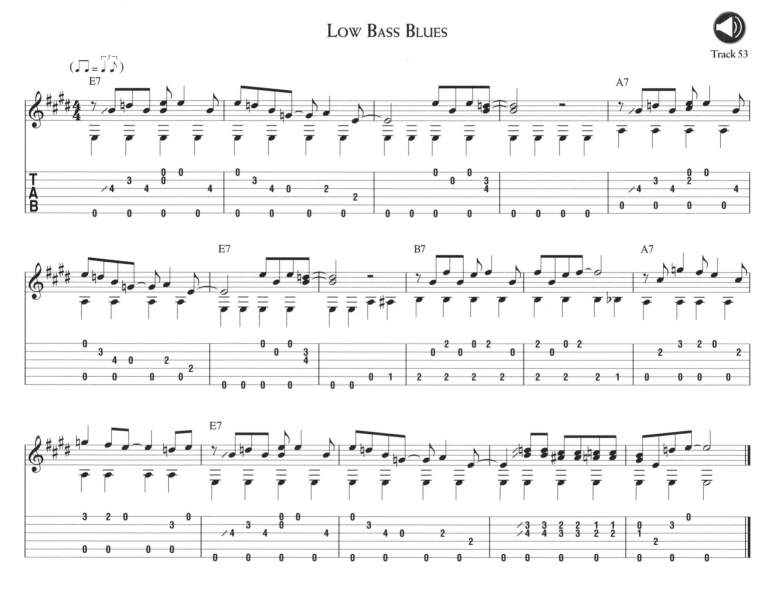

SONGS WITH MONOTONIC BASS FINGERPICKING

• "Hey Hey"—Big Bill Broonzy and Eric Clapton

• "Ain't It Hard"—Mance Lipscomb

• "Baby Please Don't Go"—Lightnin' Hopkins

• "Big Love" (Acoustic), "Rhiannon"—Fleetwood Mac

CHAPTER 14: FINGERSTYLE GUITAR AND ACCOMPANIMENT

Fingerstyle guitar is a more advanced approach to fingerpicking than anything we've covered up to this point. And yet, all of the previous fingerpicking chapters—including the basic fingerpicking lesson—can be considered a part of fingerstyle guitar. In essence, fingerstyle playing encompasses many types of fingerpicking patterns, but its underlying result is beyond patterns; sometimes you'll pick in patterns, and sometimes you'll break out of those patterns entirely.

Whether you're accompanying your voice with fingerstyle guitar or playing a solo fingerstyle piece with no vocal, you'll almost always have a melody to play on the guitar, and that's generally what causes you to break out of patterns. So in this chapter, we'll focus on working up a short fingerstyle piece called "Columbia Gorge." In the process, we'll be training our fingers to break out of patterns and get comfortable playing fingerstyle guitar.

FILLING IN THE SPACES

One of the main jobs in fingerstyle guitar is playing a melody while also learning how to fill in the spaces between that melody. You want the song to continue moving forward, whether the melody is active or pausing. Let's start by looking at the first melodic line from "Columbia Gorge."

Track 54
00:00

Now we'll fill things out with a bass line. Notice how the melody slows down over the course of that phrase. Because of that, I don't need a whole lot to drive the melody in the first measure, so I'll start with minimal bass. Then I'll speed the bass up as things progress so I can fill out the spaces that start to happen in the rhythm. If that curved line over the second and third notes is new to you, it's called a *hammer-on*. Use your middle finger to "hammer" onto the second fret without plucking (see **Chapter 17: Hammer-ons, Pull-offs, Slides, and Bends** for more on how to play hammer-ons).

Track 54
00:08

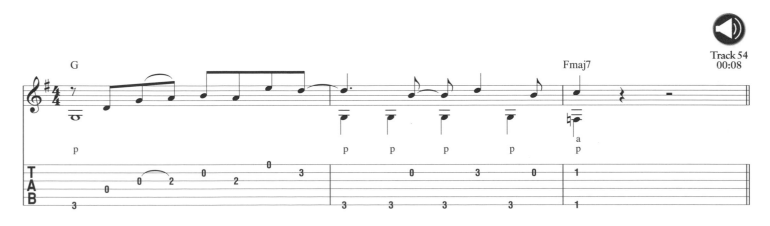

At this point, I'm playing a monotonic bass pattern in measure 2, but it doesn't sound quite right. What I really want is the flowing feel of the melody in the first measure. So instead of solid bass notes throughout, I'll try a flowing set of notes in the first part of measure 2 to make things sound less plodding:

Track 54
00:18

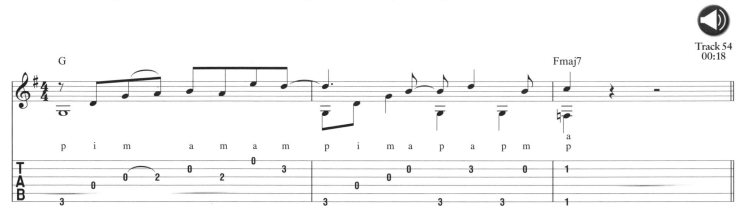

> ## TIP: Notating Fingerstyle Guitar
>
> Notice how the added filler notes in measure 2 of our third example are played with the index and middle fingers, but their stems are joined with the thumb's bass note on beat 1. In previous chapters, only thumb notes had stems pointing down, but there's more going on in fingerstyle guitar, so those notes have to go somewhere, and I've included them with the bass part. Because of this, the full value of some notes aren't always shown; for instance, that bass note on beat 1 really should ring out until the next bass note on beat 3. Fingerstyle songs often have notes ringing out like this, and it's important to keep that in mind when you play a piece. If you can also listen to a recording of a song, it will always help you know which notes ring out. Sometimes a note between the tablature and notation indicates that *everything* rings out ("*let ring throughout*"), but it's not always included.
>
> You'll occasionally see *another* set (or even two more sets) of notes floating in between the bass note (commonly referred to as "voices"), allowing the bass line and melody to each have their own set of notes. While this method ends up being more accurate because you can see how long each note needs to ring out, the sheer number of notes and "layers" of notes can be much more intimidating and difficult to read.

Once we reach that Fmaj7 chord in our melody, we have a new problem. That melody note holds for almost two measures and needs some serious filling in:

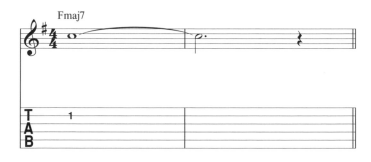

Track 55
00:00

To keep the flowing feel of our melody going, let's keep the eighth-note pulse going, like this:

Track 55
00:07

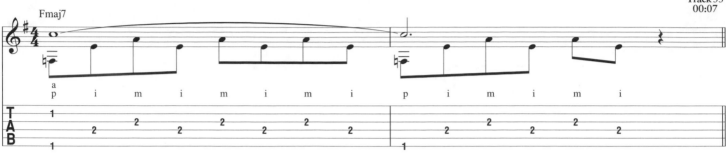

Now, there's nothing wrong with this line, but I heard another complementary line that I just had to include:

Track 55
00:15

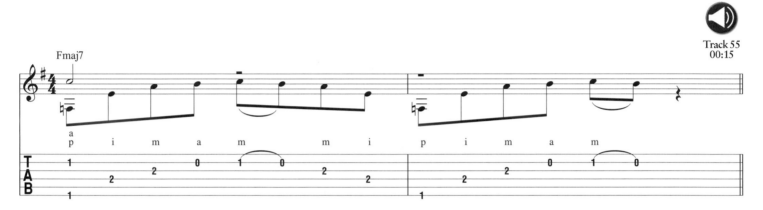

Notice how this one flows a little more like the original melody, but it's not entirely better than the previous example. Since this line's filler notes move up to the second string, the melody note ends before it really should. But our countermelody includes the melody note in it, so if we keep that countermelody slightly lower in volume, we can still highlight, while not taking too much away from, the melody line.

Moving on, the melody of our song goes here:

Track 56
00:00

SECTION III: Fingerpicking

As I've been doing, I'll add bass and filler notes to fill in the eighth-note subdivisions, which will continue to move this song forward in the same flowing fashion:

Again, I've allowed the harmony notes to creep up to the same string as the melody at times, and you can see how that truncates the length of those melody notes. But since the harmony notes are the same as the melody, it doesn't take as much away from the melody in this passage as the countermelody in the previous line did. And, while we're not playing consistent patterns, note how that rolling p–i–m–a pattern holds down most of the third and fourth measures.

TIP: Bring Out the Melody with Volume Control

One trap that fingerstyle guitarists often fall into is playing all their parts at the same volume which ends up sounding like a bunch of jumbled notes! Make sure you hear your melody notes standing out from the bass line and fill-in notes. Do whatever you need to do to bring that melody out: you may need to lighten your touch on the background parts, or you may need to dig in harder for the melody.

ADD DIFFERENT TEXTURES

So far, we've been filling out our fingerstyle arrangement by adding bass and harmony in a way that fills out nearly every eighth-note subdivision. In this song, that's worked great for keeping the flowing feeling of the melody moving along, even when a melody note is not playing. And, while we've been working around the melody, we've also been inadvertently training our fingers to bust out of patterns.

But there are many other textures that fingerstyle guitarists use in their pieces. One way you can add a different texture is by harmonizing with *double stops* (two notes played together), as I do here in the second measure:

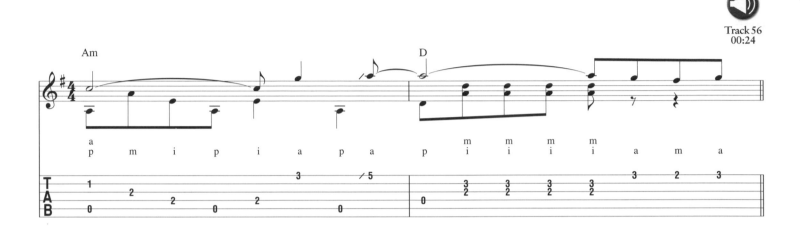

Track 56
00:24

Another common way to add texture to fingerstyle arrangements is to add *harmonics*. **Chapter 10** has a more detailed look at how to play harmonics, but briefly, you follow these three steps to sound a harmonic: 1) lightly touch a string in a specific place *directly above the fretwire* with your fretting hand, 2) pluck the string with your picking hand, and 3) quickly lift your fretting hand from the string. The most common places to play harmonics are over the fifth, seventh, and twelfth frets.

I've used harmonics in "Columbia Gorge" as a textural ending to the song:

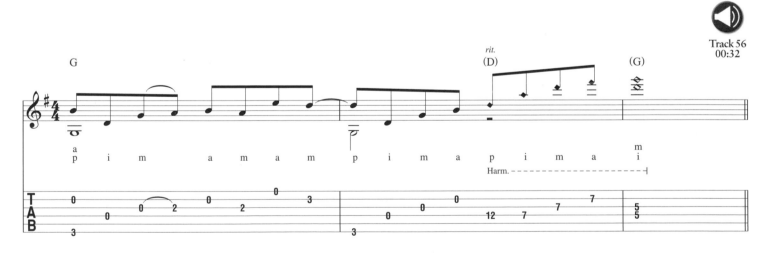

Track 56
00:32

Notice how I reach up with my thumb to pluck the first harmonic on beat 3 of measure 2. Also note the "*rit.*" marking in the example, which stands for *ritardando* (often shortened to "*ritard*"). This is another Italian word that indicates you slow down. Slowing down is a great way to end a piece, but it's also handy when you have a difficult technique, like harmonics, to slow down and cheat a little!

Now let's put all of "Columbia Gorge" together. If you look at the transcription, you can see we've already played most of the song. The only part we haven't seen yet is the stretch from measures 11–17. One move to watch out for happens across measures 11–12, where you have to barre the fifth fret with your index finger for the Am7 chord, then quickly slide up to the seventh fret to play a four-fingered G/B chord. You can leave your hand in place and simply lift your pinky finger off the string to reach the melody note at the end of measure 12, and notice how the picking pattern reverses itself at the beginning of measures 13, 15, and 17. Notice the *two rit.* markings at the end of the piece, and also notice the "*a tempo*" marking in the third to last measure, which means that you resume the original tempo (rhythm) of the piece. So you slow down after the first "*rit.*," then speed back up to the original pace at the "*a tempo*" marking, and slow it down again at the following "*rit.*"

COLUMBIA GORGE

Track 57

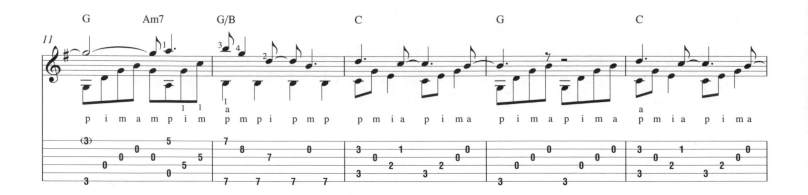

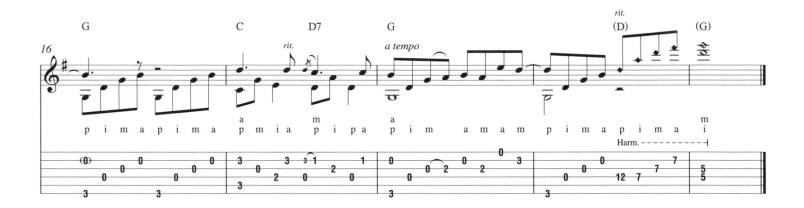

SONGS WITH FINGERSTYLE ACCOMPANIMENT OR SOLO FINGERSTYLE GUITAR

· "Fire and Rain"–James Taylor (fingerstyle accompaniment)

· "Mystery"–Willy Porter (fingerstyle accompaniment)

· "Which Will"–Nick Drake (fingerstyle accompaniment)

· "Aerial Boundaries"–Michael Hedges (solo fingerstyle)

· "Turning: Turning Back"–Alex de Grassi (solo fingerstyle)

· "L'Alchimiste"–Pierre Bensusan (solo fingerstyle)

SECTION IV:
LEAD

The term "lead guitar" often evokes an image of an electric guitarist frantically picking a solo on their knees in a huge stadium. But acoustic guitarists can play lead lines just as nifty as electric guitarists (even if they're not on their knees). Any time you play a single-note line and you're the focal point, you're playing lead guitar. It can be an improvised solo, but it can also be a scripted or signature lick of a song. And you don't have to be relegated to playing only single-note lines, either. Plenty of leads are sculpted with double stops or chordal phrases. In this section, we'll explore several scales and see how we can use them to come up with our own licks. We'll also develop our improvisation skills by playing over jam tracks so that we can play leads over chord progressions.

CHAPTER 15: THE MINOR PENTATONIC SCALE

Lead guitar is such a huge topic that you could write an encyclopedia's worth of information about it! But if you play guitar, almost every lead-playing journey starts with the minor pentatonic scale. The *minor pentatonic* scale is a five-note scale equally at home in blues, rock, jazz, country, or pop music. The unusual name is derived from the Greek word "*penta*" (which means "five') and "tonic" (which means "note"). The intervals in the scale make it "minor" (see the gray box on **Minor Pentatonic Scale Theory**). In a nutshell, the minor pentatonic scale works well over minor chord progressions with the same letter name—i.e., an E minor pentatonic scale over a song in the key of E minor. But, one great thing about the minor pentatonic scale is that it also works well over some major chord progressions, and it's especially common to use it over any blues progression, whether major or minor.

TIP: MINOR PENTATONIC SCALE THEORY

The minor pentatonic scale is a five-note scale based on the *minor scale*. More precisely, the minor pentatonic scale contains choice notes of the minor scale; while the minor scale uses seven notes, the minor pentatonic scale uses five of those notes: the root, ♭3rd, 4th, 5th, and ♭7th degrees. On your guitar, a ♭3rd is a three-fret distance on one string, a 4th is a five-fret distance, a 5th is a seven-fret distance, and a ♭7th is a ten-fret distance. While you can map these distances out on one string (below, left), the scale falls much more easily across a set of strings with two notes per string (below, right).

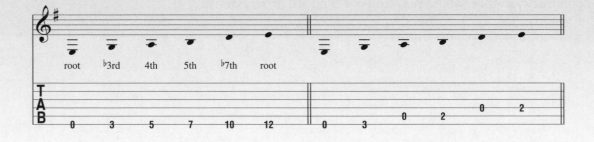

For more on these scale degrees and intervals, see **Chapter 20: The Minor Scale**.

MINOR PENTATONIC SCALE IN OPEN POSITION

Here's an E minor pentatonic scale in open position (down at the nut of the guitar):

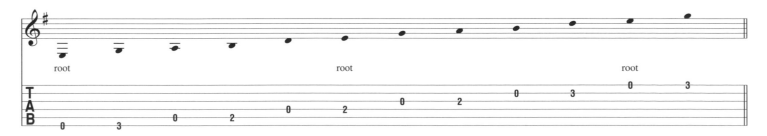

Practice this scale up and down until your fingers know where to go without having to think about it. Once you're familiar with it, you're ready to start soloing! Now, while you can play lead lines by improvising with the notes of this scale, a great place to start is by learning and creating your own *licks*—short lead lines that you can use as musical "words" to craft your own solos. A lick can be almost anything. For instance, here's a little lick on the top two strings. If this sounds familiar to you, it's because it's very similar to the lick that kicks off Eric Clapton's "Layla."

Track 58
00:00

Once you have a repertoire of licks under your fingers, you can string them together to craft your own musical "sentences." For instance, here's a little lick on the top two strings:

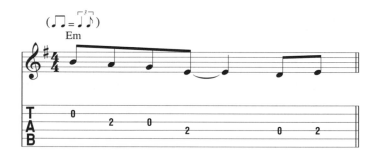

Track 58
00:07

And here's another lick on the middle three strings:

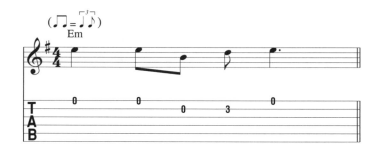

Track 58
00:14

By adding just one note, you can join these two licks together into a longer phrase:

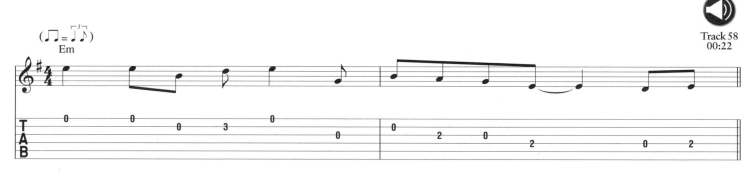

Track 58
00:22

One common trap many guitarists fall into is running up and down the scale during their solos; but instead of sounding like a solo, this ends up sounding like someone practicing their scales! You can avoid this by skipping scale notes (jumping around) and by adding rhythmic variations into your lines. You don't have to modify much to do this. Check out this line, which sounds like a scale:

Track 59
00:00

Now by simply leaving out the middle notes, we've introduced a jump *and* a rhythmic variation. The following stripped-down line sounds a lot more like a lick than a scale:

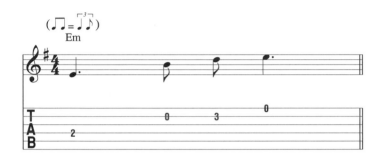

Track 59
00:07

THE MOVEABLE "BOX" SHAPE

The E minor pentatonic scale we learned is great for playing in Em down at the nut, but what if we want to play in other keys? If we move that same E minor pentatonic shape up five frets, we get an A minor pentatonic scale. The only difference here is that we have to fret the lower note in each pair:

Sometimes a fretboard pattern helps us visualize the shape more easily, so this is how these notes look on your fretboard, with the root notes circled:

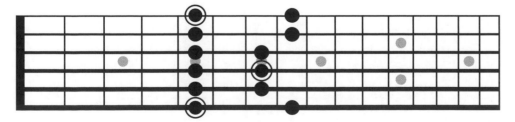

SECTION IV: Lead

Once you're in this position, you can play any licks you know from the E minor pentatonic scale in A now—just transfer them up to this shape. Here's the last lick we played, but this time it's moved up to our A minor pentatonic position:

Track 59
00:14

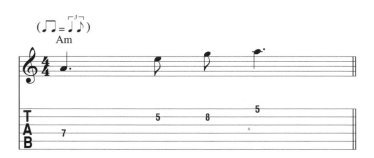

And here's the longer phrase we built by stringing two licks together:

Track 60
00:00

The beauty of this moveable minor pentatonic shape is that we can transfer it to any other key. Want to play that last lick in G minor? Just slide it down two frets:

Track 60
00:10

If you want to play it in B♭ minor, just slide your index finger up to the sixth fret:

Track 60
00:20

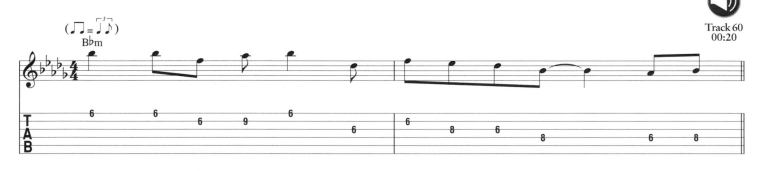

OTHER MOVEABLE SHAPES

The moveable "box" shape we just learned is the most common minor pentatonic shape; you could play countless solos with it and many guitarists never leave it. But there are also four other moveable minor pentatonic shapes.

Before we learn the other shapes, let's move back to A minor and revisit the moveable pentatonic "box." For the purposes of keeping things straight, we'll call this "Pattern 1."

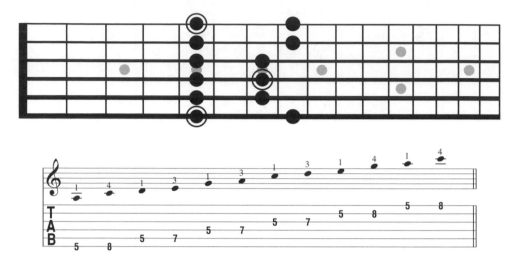

Now let's look at our second moveable minor pentatonic shape—Pattern 2:

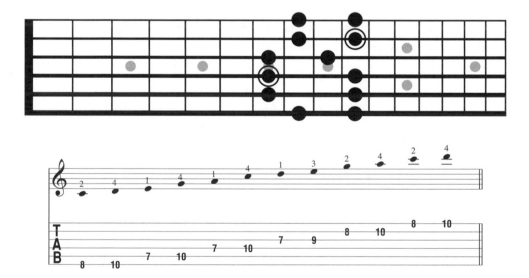

Check out how all the notes are still the same as they were in Pattern 1; we've just shifted up one note in the scale. We can play one more note up the scale than we could in Pattern 1, but we've also lost the lowest note from Pattern 1. Since we have the same notes as Pattern 1, we can still play that familiar two-measure phrase from earlier in the chapter. It might feel a little funny now, though, since our fingers play those notes in different places:

104   SECTION IV: Lead

Now let's look at Pattern 3 of our minor pentatonic scale:

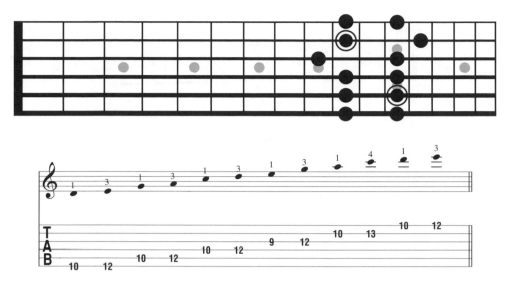

To get familiar with the shape, here's our two-measure phrase in Pattern 3:

Track 61
00:10

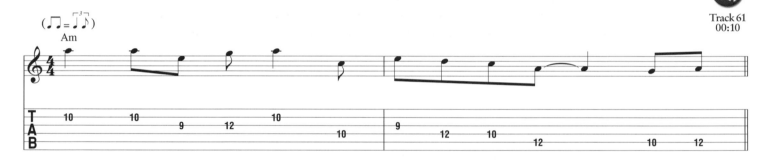

And here's Pattern 4. If you don't have a cutaway, this one's pretty tough to reach:

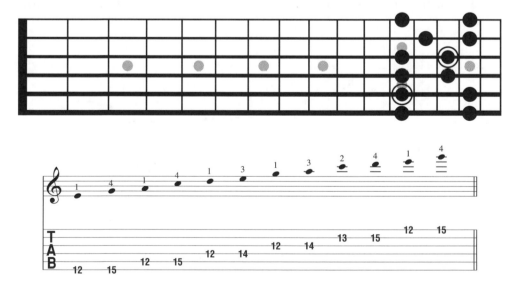

Again, see how that two-measure phrase feels way up in Pattern 4:

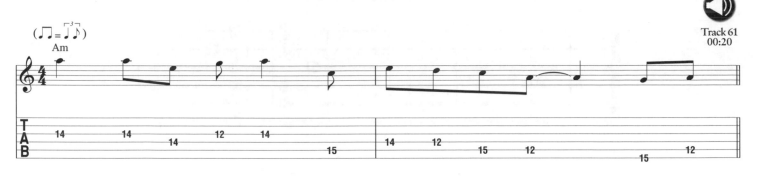

Now we have one more pattern, but we're so high up the neck that we can't reach it unless we have a cutaway. So let's try Pattern 5 *down* one octave in second position:

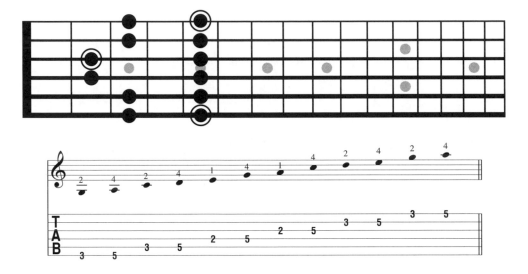

We can still play our two-measure phrase in Pattern 5, though the phrase reaches our highest note:

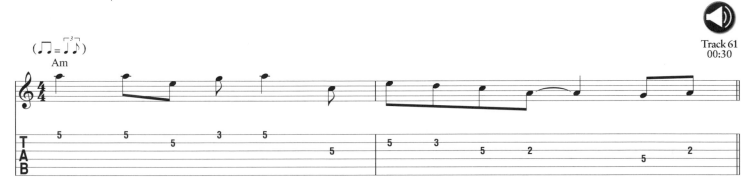

Of course, it's near impossible to memorize these patterns by playing them once or twice, so bookmark these pages and practice the patterns whenever you have a chance. Start with Pattern 1 and branch out from there, memorizing one at a time. Before you know it, you'll have them all under your fingers, but it will take some concentrated practicing over a period of time.

SHIFTING BETWEEN POSITIONS

Once you're comfortable with each position, it's time to practice moving between positions. Why would you want to do that? Well, it gives you access to more notes, along with the flexibility to move around the fretboard (instead of getting caught in one position). You'll find that licks have a different sound too when played in different areas of the neck. If you want a stinging, trebly tone, you'll want to play on the thinner strings nearer the nut. For a thick, throaty sound, use the lower strings higher up the neck.

It's true that you can play many things in one position, and we just played the exact same two-measure phrase in every pattern. But not all phrases are alike; many will work best in one pattern, and some sound better when they're played across several patterns. We'll get into this further in **Chapter 17: Hammer-ons, Pull-offs, Slides, and Bends**.

Let's start by taking a bird's-eye view of all the patterns. From this fretboard diagram, you can see that each pattern shares notes with two other patterns—one below and one above. I've shown one set of patterns, but they continue on below and above—the bottom of pattern 5 is also the top of pattern 4, etc.

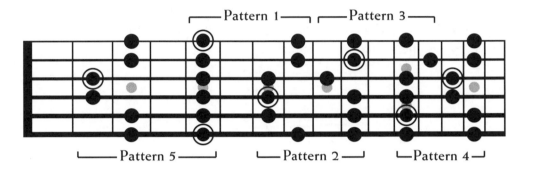

The most common patterns to join are Patterns 1 and 2, and this move is one of the easiest ways to play across these two patterns:

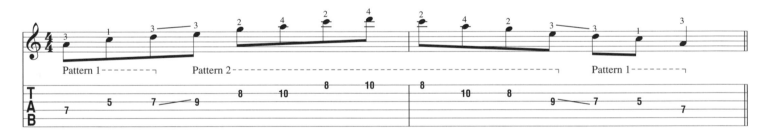

As you can see, the third finger plays the third string, seventh fret in pattern 1. Since the third finger also plays the third string, ninth fret of Pattern 2, you can move between patterns by sliding this finger up two frets and continuing in pattern 2. To switch back to Pattern 1, just reverse the process.

Following this same philosophy of using a finger to shift positions, you could also slide between Patterns 1 and 2 with your index finger on the third string, like this:

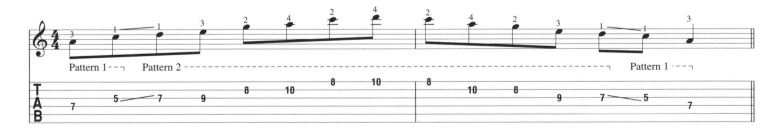

Sometimes, you can shift between positions by sliding with a finger that *doesn't* share a note in both patterns. In this lick, we slide from Pattern 2 up to Pattern 3 with the fourth finger. The fourth finger usually doesn't play that high E note in Pattern 2, but it works fine as a transition. We'll pop into the standard Pattern 3 fingering by playing the following D with our index finger, and we're in position to play the final notes with standard Pattern 3 fingerings.

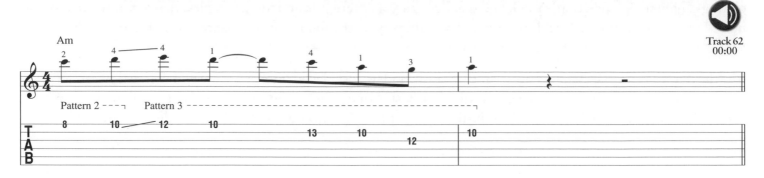

Other times, a lick will dictate that you change your fingering a little for one of the patterns. In this little lick, sliding your index finger down from Pattern 1 to Pattern 5 leaves you fretting the first and third frets with your first and third fingers, instead of the typical second and fourth fingers:

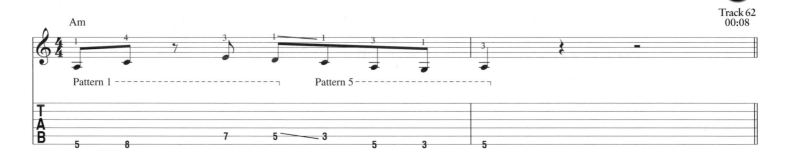

Another way to join patterns is by spreading out the fingers of your fretting hand and grabbing notes with consecutive fingers to move into another position. This lick starts in Pattern 4 and then quickly moves into Pattern 5. Notice how this one-note-per-finger rule applies on the second, third, and fourth notes of the lick. That twelfth-fret G note is a part of both patterns, but neither pattern uses the second finger here; this is the note where we shift between positions via our one-finger-per note method:

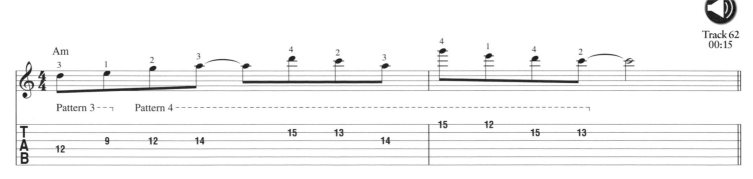

As you can see, there are plenty of ways to switch between patterns, and we've explored a few. Try applying these concepts to the patterns in your own playing by shifting in different places than we've done in the past few examples.

BLUES SOLO AND JAM

Now it's time for a little fun! Let's practice the licks we've learned and a few others in a blues solo:

MINOR BLUES SOLO

Track 63

TIP: MINOR BLUES CHORD PROGRESSION

Our blues jam and solo in this lesson is in the key of A minor, and the basic progression for a 12-bar blues in Am is: Am (four measures)–Dm (two measures)–Am (two measures)–Em (one measure)–Dm (one measure)–Am (two measures). We've dressed our progression up a little by going back to Em in the last measure, and many blues tunes do this. In fact, that final Em chord addition is often played at many different places: from just before the downbeat of the final measure to midway through the final measure, depending on the tune. There are many other 12-bar blues variations out there, but this knowledge should help you follow many of them. Once you know about chord functions (in **Chapter 19**), you can transfer this progression to any key, and we'll discuss that at the end of **Chapter 20**.

Now it's your turn! Throw in the licks from the previous solo, some throughout this lesson, come up with some of your own, or even practice a few scale runs over the following minor blues progression.

MINOR BLUES JAM

Track 64

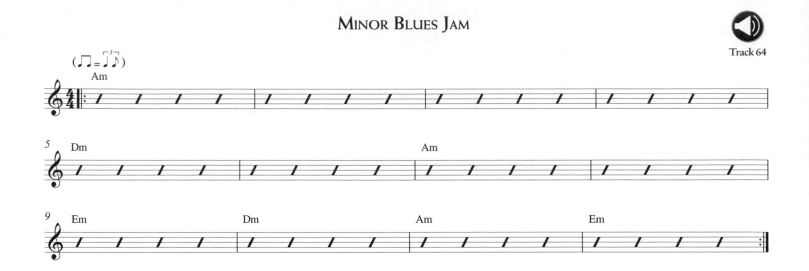

CHAPTER 16: THE MAJOR PENTATONIC SCALE

While the minor pentatonic scale has a bluesy, soulful, and sometimes "sad" sound, the *major pentatonic* scale has a "happy" or "up" sound. It works great over major-key songs and it's a nice scale to have under your fingers to contrast with the darker sound of the minor pentatonic scale.

TIP: Major Pentatonic Scale Theory

The *major pentatonic* scale is a five-note scale based on the *major scale*. More precisely, the major pentatonic scale contains choice notes of the major scale. The major scale contains seven notes, and the major pentatonic scale uses five of those notes: the root, 2nd, 3rd, 5th, and 6th degrees. On your guitar, a major 2nd is a two-fret distance on one string, a major 3rd is a four-fret distance, a 5th is a seven-fret distance, and a major 6th is a nine-fret distance. While you can map these distances out on one string (below, left), the scale falls much more easily across a set of strings with two notes per string (below, right).

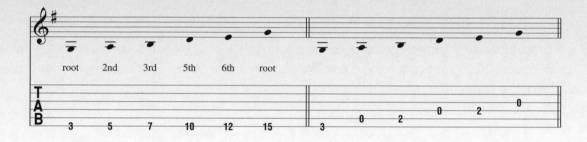

For more on these scale degrees and intervals, see **Chapter 19: The Major Scale**.

MAJOR PENTATONIC SCALE IN OPEN POSITION

Let's start by playing a G major pentatonic scale in open position (at the nut of your guitar):

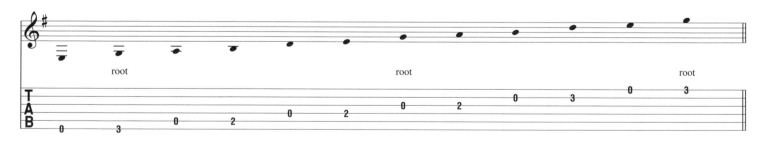

Does this scale seem familiar? You may have noticed that it's *exactly the same* as the E minor pentatonic scale we used at the beginning of **Chapter 15**. How can this be? Well, every major scale has its *relative minor* scale, and every minor scale has its *relative major* scale. As you can see here, the E minor pentatonic scale and the G major pentatonic scale are the relative major/minor scales to each other. So they have exactly the same notes, but they actually *are* different scales because they start at different places. Notice how the starting (*root*) note for the E minor pentatonic scale was the open sixth string E note, while the root note for the G major pentatonic scale is the third fret G note on the sixth string. So, the difference is in the *context* of those notes, and you can hear that in the following lick:

Track 65
00:00

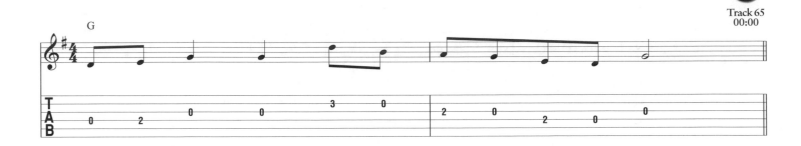

When you're crafting lines with the major pentatonic scale, remember what we learned in the minor pentatonic chapter: running scales *sounds* like practicing scales—not like playing a solo. A line like this might sound too much like running up and down the scale:

Track 65
00:08

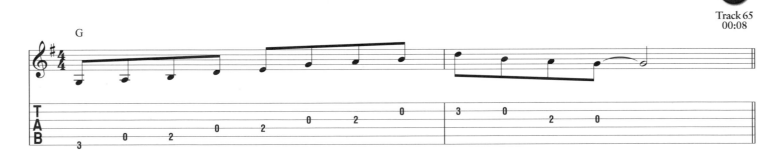

So make sure to mix it up. Leave out a few notes, stretch out the rhythms of the other notes, and you have this:

Track 65
00:16

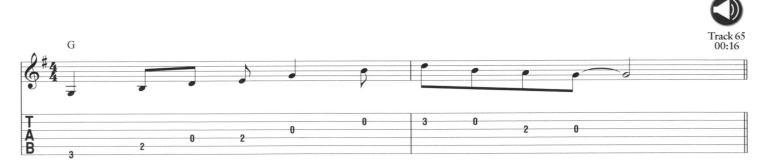

SECTION IV: Lead

Then again, *sometimes* running a scale can make a pretty cool lick, like the following line, which is very similar to the opening of the Allman Brothers' "Ramblin' Man."

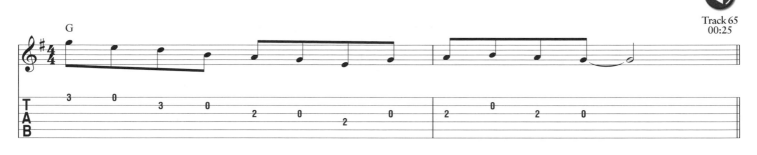

Track 65
00:25

These kinds of licks are usually the exception to the rule, so remember to mix it up every so often by varying the rhythm and skipping around a bit. Ultimately, you're trying to create phrases—similar to a spoken conversation. Just as someone's speech has natural pauses, starts, stops, and varied rhythms, so should your licks.

MOVEABLE MAJOR PENTATONIC SCALES

The major pentatonic scale has five moveable shapes, just like the minor pentatonic scale. And since these scales share the same notes, you really already know all five shapes! Of course, since the starting place of each scale is in a different place, it's good to practice these major pentatonic shapes separately from the minor pentatonic ones, keeping their root notes in mind. So let's slide our G shape up so that the root note falls on the eighth-fret C note:

C Major Pentatonic Pattern 5

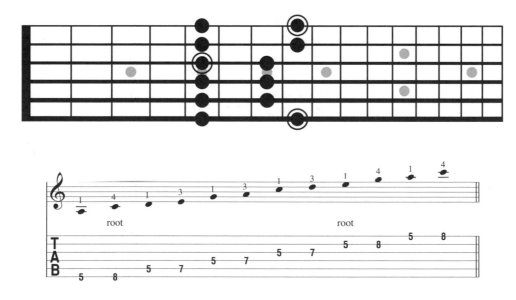

Notice how I called this Pattern 5 instead of Pattern 1. There's a reason for that, which we'll explore more fully in **Chapter 21: Mixing Major and Minor Pentatonic Scales.** For now, let's focus on learning the shapes, and we'll see why each one is labeled this way when we reach **Chapter 21.**

Here are the other four shapes, starting with Pattern 1:

C Major Pentatonic Pattern 1

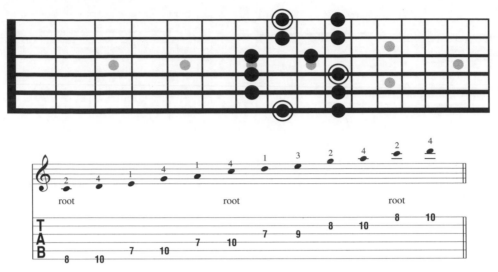

C Major Pentatonic Pattern 2

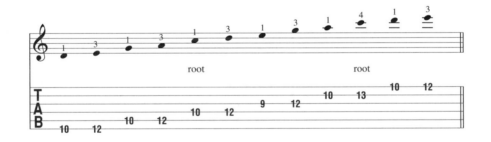

C Major Pentatonic Pattern 3

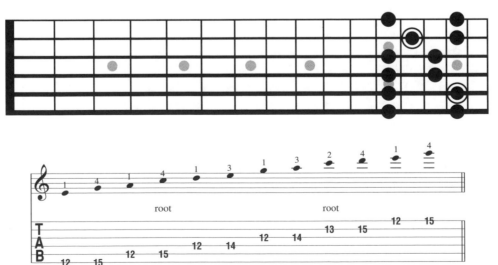

SECTION IV: Lead

C Major Pentatonic Pattern 4

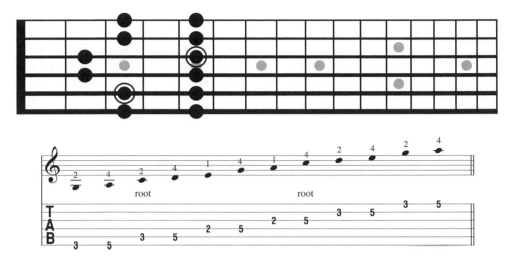

Get to know these shapes inside and out, and try playing as many licks as possible in different positions. Here's one using Pattern 1:

Track 66
00:00

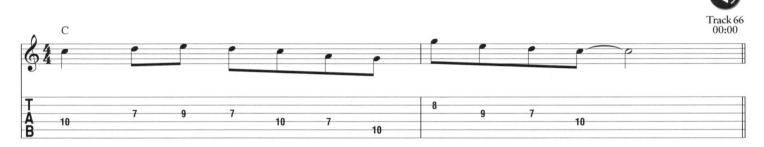

You can play this lick in all the positions. Try transferring it to each position on your own.

Not all licks will work in every position, though. Sometimes moving the lick up or down an octave will allow you to play it in another position. For instance, let's try this lick in Pattern 2:

Track 66
00:08

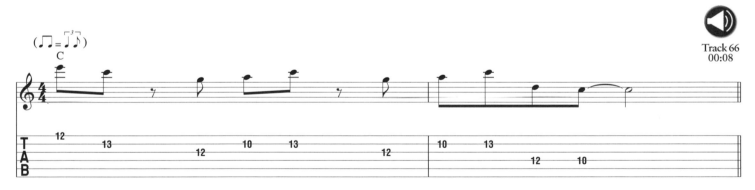

It's too high for us to play in Pattern 4, but if we move it down an octave, it works fine there in Pattern 4:

Track 66
00:16

TIP: ROLL OVER

You may notice that it's a bit more difficult to play this lick with Pattern 4, because all of those notes in a row on the fifth fret are difficult to grab. One trick for grabbing consecutive notes on the same fret is to *roll* your fretting finger from one string to the next. For instance, on the first note of the lick, flatten your index finger a little bit and fret the E note with the flattened part of the finger. Once you've played the first note, roll your index finger up onto its tip. In this one motion, you'll let go of the second string, and the tip of your finger will simultaneously fret the fifth fret on the third string—all ready to play the next note! Rolling in the next measure is much more difficult—from the third string to the fifth string—so don't worry if you can't immediately master it. Slow things down and eventually you'll be able to work it up to speed.

SHIFTING BETWEEN POSITIONS

Here is how all of the patterns fit together on the fretboard:

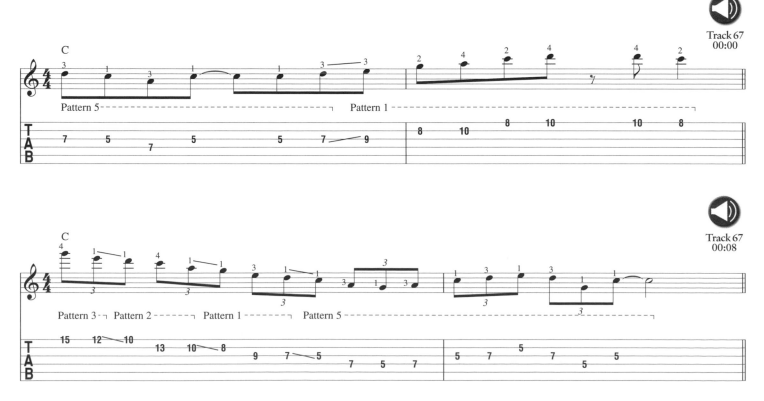

We can switch between them the same way we did with the minor pentatonic scales—by sliding a finger or using by using our "one-note-per-finger" trick. Here are several licks that move between positions using these techniques; the first two use a sliding finger, and the third uses one-note-per-finger to move into another position. Practice these examples and come up with other ways of shifting between all positions. There are many possibilities!

116   SECTION IV: Lead

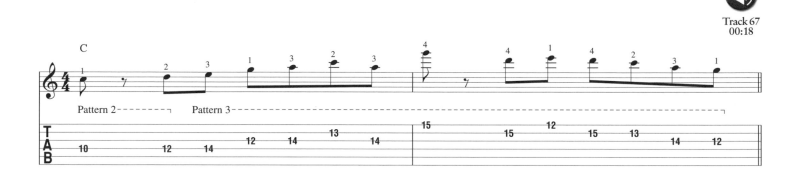

ACOUSTIC SOUTHERN ROCK JAM

Now it's time for us to jam with the major pentatonic scale! Here's a solo with a few new licks for you to try out:

ACOUSTIC SOUTHERN ROCK SOLO

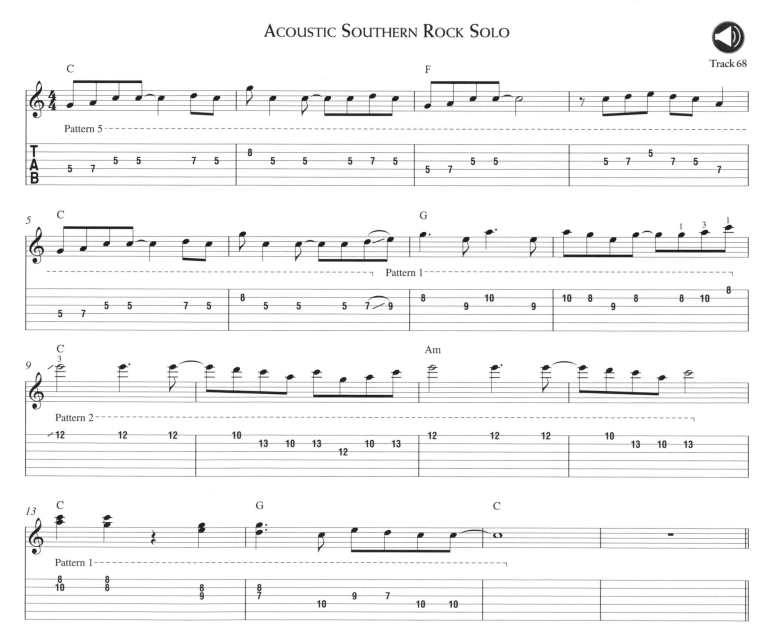

Check out the shift from Pattern 1 to Pattern 2 at the end of measure 8. You can see I've changed my fingering on those last three notes to make the slide up to Pattern 2 a bit easier. Also notice the double-stop phrase in measures 13–14. These are a common sound in major pentatonic jams, and we'll spice them up a bit more in the next chapter (**Chapter 17: Hammer-ons, Pull-offs, and Slides**).

Now come up with your own solo and licks over the jam track.

ACOUSTIC SOUTHERN ROCK JAM

Track 69

SECTION IV: Lead

CHAPTER 17: HAMMER-ONS, PULL-OFFS, SLIDES, AND BENDS

If scales are the foundation of soloing, then hammer-ons, pull-offs, slides, and bends are soloing's custom moulding, granite countertops, and hardwood floors; they're the special details that take a solo from ordinary and make it sound great. Without further ado, let's dig into these techniques!

HAMMER-ONS

In written music, a *hammer-on* is notated with a slur over (or under) two notes. As you might guess, you play a hammer-on by playing one note and then "hammering" onto the next one with your fret hand (the second note is not articulated by your picking hand). In the following example, play the open third string, and then use your fret hand's index or middle finger to hammer onto the second fret:

Track 70
00:00

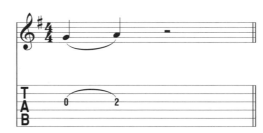

Make sure your finger lands firmly on the fretboard with the tip of the finger—just as you'd fret any other note. You might have to experiment with the amount of force you use to try and make the note the same volume as the previous one. Now let's try playing an E minor pentatonic scale with hammer-ons:

Track 70
00:06

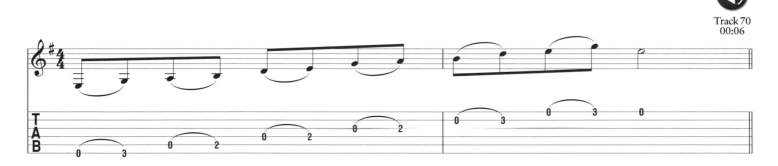

To play a hammer-on further up the neck, you'll have to fret the first note with one finger, pluck the string, and hammer on with another. To get a feel for it, try this one out:

Track 70
00:16

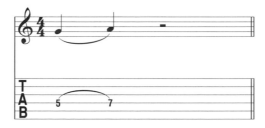

Let's practice a few of these using an A minor pentatonic scale at the fifth fret:

Track 70
00:22

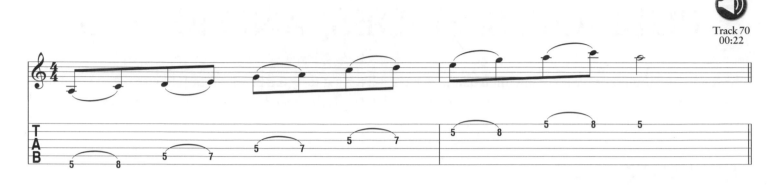

Now try this phrase. First, play it with the hammer-ons, and then play through it without hammer-ons (by picking every note). Comparing the two can show you how much a few little hammer-ons can add to a phrase:

Track 71
00:00

One nifty trick is to use hammer-ons as grace notes. A *grace note* is a very quick note that doesn't have any defined value. You either play a grace note *shortly before* a beat, or else you play a grace note *right on the beat*, but it happens so quickly that you immediately move to the note written on the beat. Here's how it looks and sounds:

Track 71
00:14

Grace-note hammer-ons work great on single-note lines, but you'll often hear them in double-stop lines as well. Check out how much better the double-stop lick from our major pentatonic solo in **Chapter 16** sounds with grace notes:

Track 71
00:21

Now try integrating hammer-ons into your own licks. To get you started, let's see how the opening lick from our major pentatonic solo in **Chapter 16** sounds with one carefully placed hammer-on.

Track 71
00:30

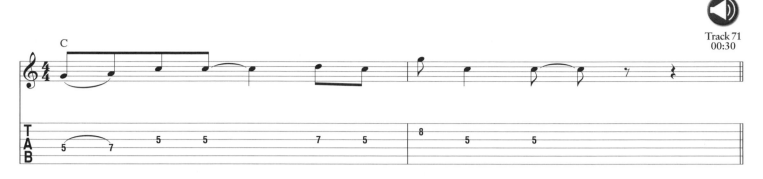

PULL-OFFS

In written music, a *pull-off* is notated with a slur over (or under) two notes—just like a hammer-on. The way you tell the two apart is that a pull-off moves from a higher note to a lower note, whereas a hammer-on goes the other way (from a lower note to a higher note). To play the pull-off below, fret the A note on the third string with your index or middle finger, pluck the string, and then quickly pull your finger in a downward motion off the fret to sound the open string.

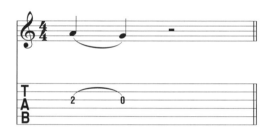

Track 72
00:00

You may find this motion a little tougher than the hammer-on. Fret the note with the fleshy part of your fingertip. That way, you'll have more reinforcement for the pull-off. If you fret the note too close to the nail, the string can slip out from under your finger as you attempt the pull-off and the next note won't sound loud enough (or at all). As you pull downward (towards the floor), also angle your finger slightly away from the fretboard so that it doesn't brush the other strings. You're, in essence, plucking the string with this fret-hand finger.

Now let's practice our pull-offs with the E minor pentatonic scale:

Track 72
00:06

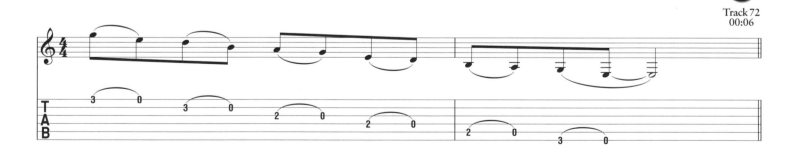

To play a pull-off up the neck, start by fretting *both* notes. Once you've plucked the string, pull off from the higher note (while leaving that lower note fretted):

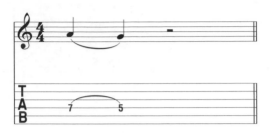

Track 72
00:16

Again, let's practice these pull-offs with the A minor pentatonic scale to get more comfortable with them:

Track 72
00:23

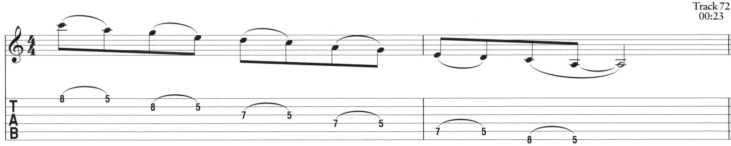

Now try using pull-offs in your own licks and riffs. Here's a simple A minor pentatonic lick to get you started:

Track 73
00:00

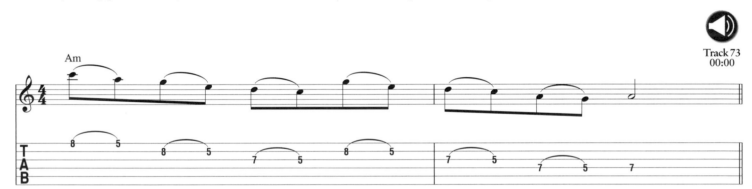

HAMMER-ONS AND PULL-OFFS TOGETHER

Hammer-ons and pull-offs sound fine on their own, but you'll often see them cropping up together in riffs and licks. See how much better this major pentatonic lick (from **Chapter 16**) sounds when we add a hammer-on and a few pull-offs:

Track 73
00:10

And, if you want to get really fancy, a nifty trick is to play hammer-on and pull-off combinations on consecutive notes. We looked at the following minor pentatonic lick back in **Chapter 15** (in E minor, rather than A minor). See how it flows much easier with the hammer-and-pull combination on beats 2 and 3.

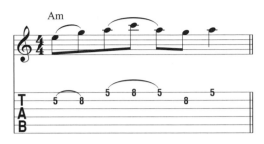

Track 73
00:20

SLIDES

Slides add fluidity to your lines and can help you shift between positions more easily. There are many ways you can use slides. First, you can slide into a note from above or below:

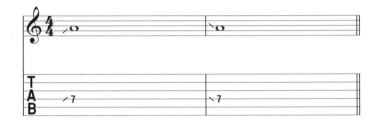

Track 74
00:00

In the previous slides, you're sliding in from an unspecified place—just slide into the target note and don't worry about where the slide starts. When a quick slide into a note *is* supposed to start in a specific place, you'll see that written with a grace note:

Track 74
00:09

You can also slide from one note to another. In these examples, pluck only the first note (the slur over the slide indicates that you only pick the first note). This is referred to as a *legato slide*.

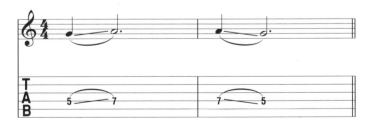

Track 74
00:19

The last type of slide we'll look at is a slide from one note to another where *both* notes are picked (there's no slur over this type of slide, indicating that you *do* pick both notes). This is referred to as a *shift slide* or a *picked* (or *plucked*) *slide*.

Track 74
00:29

Now let's try slides in a few licks. The following major pentatonic lick sounds much smoother with the slide into beat 3:

Track 75
00:00

A common minor pentatonic move shifts you from Pattern 1 up to Pattern 2 and back down again (in E minor, Pattern 1 in root position). Note that we're combining a slide with a pull-off in this lick—a very common move in blues and rock styles.

Track 75
00:07

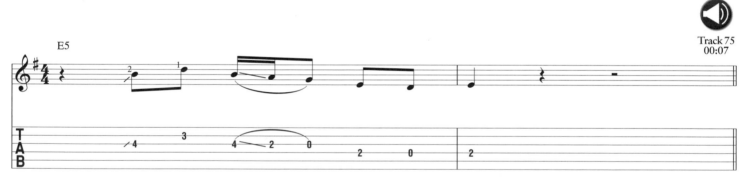

As you can see from the previous lick, slides can help you shift between positions and make those transitions sound like great licks. Here's a major pentatonic lick we looked at in **Chapter 16**. If we add slides (and pull-offs), notice how much smoother the lick sounds, and how much easier the shifting between positions feels:

Track 75
00:16

BENDS

Bends are much more difficult on acoustic guitar than on electric guitar because the strings tend to be thicker and harder to move on an acoustic. So, while bends are a common staple in electric guitar, they're not quite as common in the acoustic guitar world. But you *can* play bends on an acoustic—you just might not be able to bend as many strings as far as you can with an electric.

To bend a note, reinforce the bending finger with a few fingers. For instance, on the following bend, use your ring finger to bend the note up a *half step* (the distance of one fret), but reinforce that finger with your index and middle fingers—use *all three* to push the string upwards:

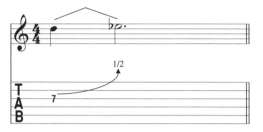

Track 76
00:00

Since the "destination note" of your bend is equal to one fret, you can check the way your bend sounds against the note a half step above, like this:

Track 76
00:07

Once you've reached the height of your bend, your bend is either over, *or* you can release it, like this:

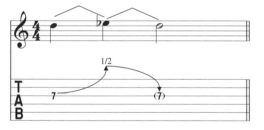

Track 76
00:18

If you quietly bend a string *before* you pluck it, and then pluck and release the note, it's called a *pre-bend*:

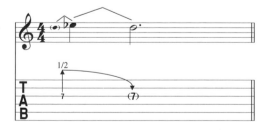

Track 76
00:25

Now let's try some bends in a few licks. This one uses a bend and release in an A minor pentatonic lick. Notice the pull-off after the bend. This is a common addition to this type of bending lick.

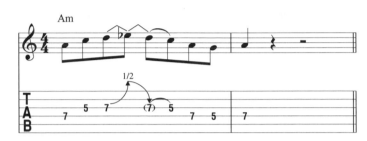

Track 76
00:33

Another common lick is to bend up a whole step (also called a "full" bend) on the second string. This one's tough because you have to bend twice the distance of the previous bend (a *whole step* is a two-fret distance). Make sure you reinforce the bend with the other fingers of your fretting hand.

Track 77
00:00

This bend crops up all over the place, and you often hear it followed by the root note on the first string, as in the following short lick:

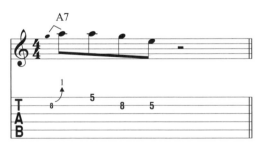

Track 77
00:06

To grab that first-string note after the bend, you'll need your index finger ready to go, so you won't be able to use it to reinforce the bend. This makes the bend a little tougher, but you'll still have your middle ring and pinky fingers pushing up on the string. You also hear this bend alternated with that first-string note (which is the same note as your bent note) for a slick repetitive sound. This one takes a bit of practice, so take your time!

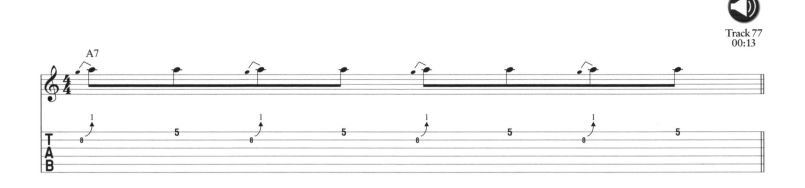

Combining all these techniques gives you unlimited options for creating licks. Here's one that uses bends, a pull-off, a hammer-on, and double stops. Barre your ring and index fingers across the seventh and fifth frets for the double stops (use your ring finger for the seventh fret and your index finger for the fifth fret).

You may have noticed that the F♯ note in the first double stop and the C♯ note we hammer onto are both not part of the minor pentatonic scale. They're actually part of the *major* pentatonic scale. Right now, we're mostly concerned with playing this lick and getting it under our fingers, but we'll explore how these extra notes come together in **Chapter 21: Mixing Major and Minor Pentatonic Scales**.

> **TIP: SHOULD I PUSH UP OR PULL DOWN ON MY BENDS?**
>
> We've been bending on the top three strings in this lesson, and we've been bending those strings by pushing up. One reason for this is that your fingers have more leverage pushing up on those top three strings. Another reason to push up—especially on the top string—is that you don't have room on the fretboard to pull down; you'll pull it right off the fretboard! (And that doesn't sound pretty.)
>
> If you bend on the lower strings, however—especially on the fifth or sixth strings—pulling down works better.

BLUES JAM

Now let's play a solo using all of our new tools—hammer-ons, pull-offs, bends, and slides. This one's in the key of G, and we'll be using the G minor pentatonic scale. While we've mostly been playing the A minor pentatonic scale, remember that all you have to do is move those same shapes down two frets to play G minor pentatonic.

There's one new trick I've thrown into this solo: *quarter-step bends*. These are smaller than half-step bends—small enough that you're not really bending to another note; just bend that string up until it sounds a little bleusy!

TIP: Vibrato

Those squiggly lines at the end of the second and sixth measures are *vibrato*—a technique that gives a note a fluttering sound. (Listen to the example to hear what this sounds like.) To play vibrato, you basically repeat quick bend-and-releases on a note. The bend is very small—a quarter-step bend or less. Practice by playing a long note and adding vibrato for as long as the note sounds.

Most steel-string guitarists play the bending vibrato we just learned, but Classical guitarists play a different type of vibrato. Instead of bending a note, classical vibrato has your finger rocking horizontally along the plane of the string—back towards the previous fret and then up towards the next fret. It's a subtler type of vibrato and it tends to work better on nylon-string guitars.

Pay attention to the fingerings that show up on a few of the notes. You'll notice that I'm using the first and third fingers on the sixth and eighth frets, instead of the second and fourth fingers—like you'd usually use on Pattern 2. This alternate fingering allows you to bend the note on the eighth fret more easily; your ring finger is much stronger than your pinky for these types of bends.

You can roll your ring finger across the top two strings at the end of measure 6 to get those eighth-fret notes. But also try the new fingering noted above the notes (using your middle finger on the second string). This is an easier way to fret this popular lick.

G Blues Solo

Track 78

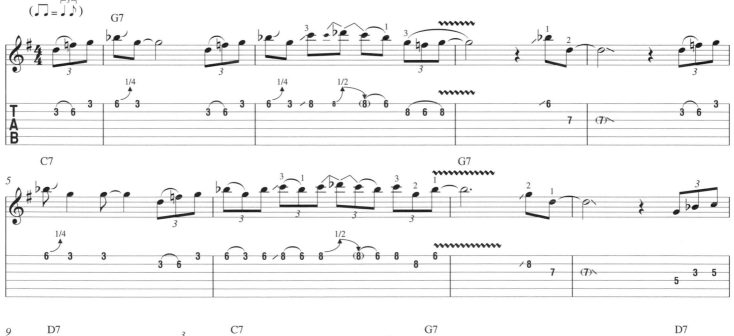

SECTION IV: Lead

Now it's your turn. Here's the jam track for our blues jam in G. Try out your own licks and make sure to practice all our new hammer-on, pull-off, slide, and bend licks:

G BLUES JAM TRACK

Track 79

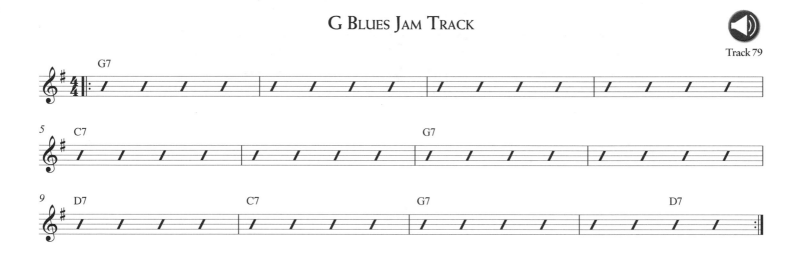

CHAPTER 18: THE BLUES SCALE

The *blues scale* is a modified minor pentatonic scale with one added note: the ♭5th. This note falls between the 4th and 5th degrees of the minor pentatonic scale and it's just discordant enough to add an extra "bluesy" sound to your solos. Its placement right between the 4th and 5th degrees of a minor pentatonic scale also means that you have three notes in a row, all one fret apart—allowing you to create some slippery sounding lines that would be difficult to simulate with an unmodified minor pentatonic scale.

Since the blues scale is so closely related to the minor pentatonic scale, it will sound great in any genre the minor pentatonic scale does (which is pretty much anything!—but especially blues and rock). You already know the minor pentatonic scale, so the blues scale is an easy addition to your toolbox. Just pop that ♭5th note between the 4th and 5th degrees of your scale patterns, and you've got a blues scale. Here's how Pattern 1 looks:

A BLUES SCALE PATTERN 1

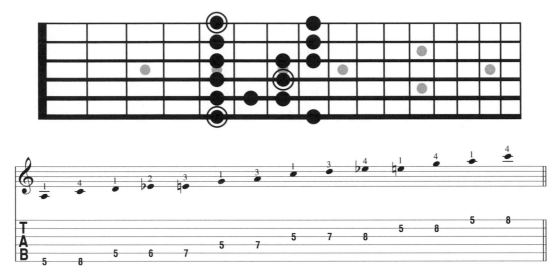

Here's a lick that uses the bluesy sound of this scale:

Track 80
00:00

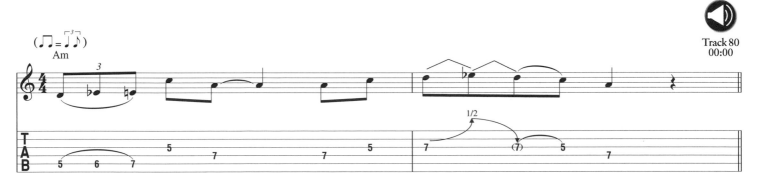

Did you notice that bend in the second measure? It's the same bend we played in **Chapter 17** and it bends up to the ♭5th note in the blues scale. (You may not have known it at the time, but you've *already* been playing the blues scale in your bends!)

The blues scale also works great using triplets:

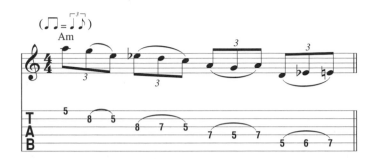

Track 80
00:12

Now try modifying some of your own minor pentatonic licks by working in this new note and see where it takes you.

ADAPT YOUR FINGERINGS

Learning the Pattern 1 blues scale is a breeze because that extra note falls easily into the four-fret span carved out by minor pentatonic Pattern 1. But when you add that single note to the other patterns, you might tie your fingers in knots trying to play them! To see what I mean, let's take a look at the Pattern 2 blues scale. If you want to play this scale without sliding or spreading your fingers, this is how you'll have to play it:

A BLUES SCALE PATTERN 2

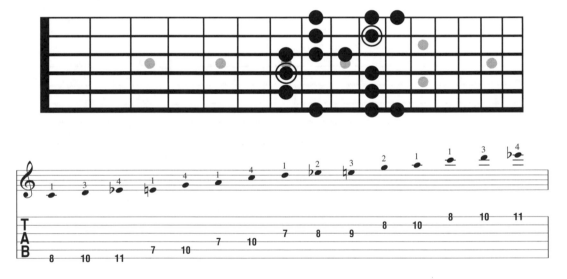

Notice how you'll have to shift your fretting hand up a fret on the first and sixth strings, and then move it down a fret when you move to any other string. But this is just one way to finger this pattern. You can also access the extra notes by sliding to them with your pinky finger. In that case, you'd use the same fingerings as the minor pentatonic scale (your middle and pinky fingers on the first and sixth strings); this lick uses slides to access the extra notes:

Track 80
00:21

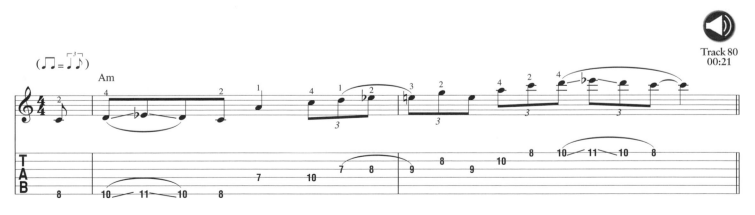

Aside from Pattern 1, Pattern 3 is the only other pattern where you won't have to adapt your minor pentatonic fingerings to access all the notes. Here's how the Pattern 3 blues scale looks:

A Blues Scale Pattern 3

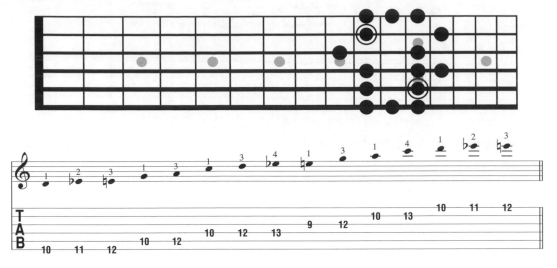

Now let's look at the Pattern 4 blues scale. To play this one without sliding, you'll have to stretch up with your pinky on the first and sixth strings:

A Blues Scale Pattern 4

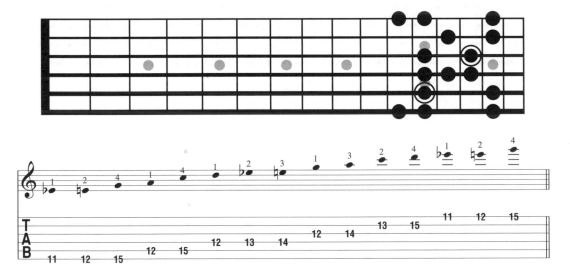

If you find this stretch a breeze—great! But if it's a little difficult, try sliding with your first finger to the extra note on the first and sixth strings, as shown in the following lick:

Track 80
00:33

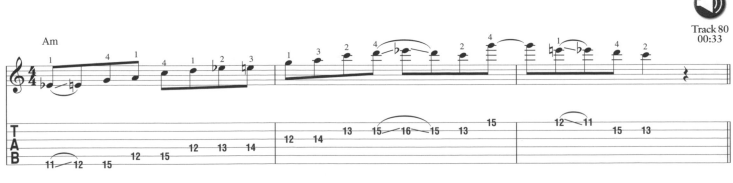

SECTION IV: Lead

It's easy to slide down with your first finger and grab those extra notes, but I threw something else in this lick: I accessed that extra blues-scale note on the *second* string by sliding up with my pinky in measure 2. The Pattern 4 blues scale I mapped out has this note on the first string, instead of the second. But it's also easily accessible on the second string, and you can also throw that into any other lick that passes through the second string.

> ### TIP: SLIDE OUT OF ANY PATTERN TO GRAB THE ♭5TH NOTE
>
> The previous Pattern 4 blues scale lick slides out of the pattern to play the ♭5th on the *second* string, instead of playing that note on the first string. You can slide out of any other blues-scale pattern to grab that ♭5th note, whenever it's a single fret away. For instance, whenever you play the 4th degree, you'll always be just one fret beneath that ♭5th note, and you can slide up one fret to grab it, even if it's out of your current pattern. That also works coming from the other direction: whenever you're parked on the 5th, you can always slide *down* one fret to the blues scale's ♭5th degree, even if it's not part of your current pattern.

Now let's look at the fifth blues-scale pattern. If we want to play the scale without sliding, we'll have to modify our fingering on the bottom two strings and use our index and ring fingers on the third and fifth frets, respectively:

A BLUES SCALE PATTERN 5

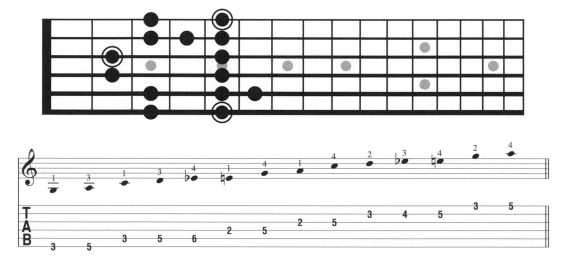

Again, you can stay in your minor pentatonic position and access the extra note on the fifth string via slides, if you prefer. Here's a lick that uses this fingering:

Track 80
00:43

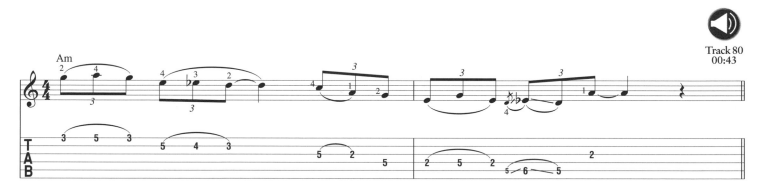

Remember that all these patterns fit together in exactly the same way for every key. If you want to play in G, slide the patterns down two frets; if you want to play in C, slide the shapes up three frets.

BLUES SCALE JAM

Let's try the blues scale out on a solo and jam over an Am blues. Our solo spends most of its time in Pattern 1, with a brief visit to Pattern 5, and a slide up to Pattern 2 for two measures, before returning to Pattern 1. One of the trickier moves happens in measure 9, with the whole-step bends followed by a quarter-step bend. Make sure to reinforce those whole-step bends with your index and middle fingers, but the quarter-step bend (and many throughout the solo) are played with the first finger, so one finger has to provide the bend all by itself. This isn't as difficult as it may look, though, because a quarter-step bend is much easier than a whole-step bend. And, while we're speaking of those whole-step bends, did you notice that we bent up to a B note, which isn't part of our A blues scale? We're less concerned with *why* it works right now, since it sounds good. But if you're curious, we'll talk about how that note fits in during **Chapter 21: Mixing Major and Minor Pentatonic Scales**.

BLUES SCALE SOLO

Track 81

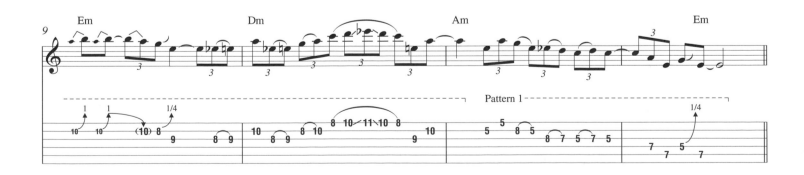

Throughout this solo, we accessed our extra blues-scale note (♭5th) via a few slides in Pattern 2. Check out how they add a slippery feel and sound to those licks. Now it's your turn! Practice your blues-scale soloing over the following jam track:

BLUES SCALE JAM TRACK

Track 82

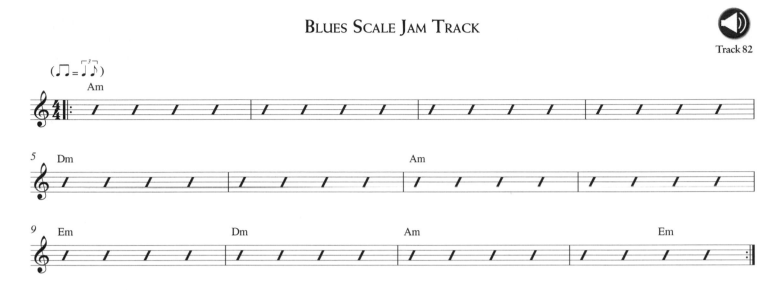

CHAPTER 19: THE MAJOR SCALE

The *major scale* is the most important scale in Western music. And when we say "Western music," we're not just talking about the soundtracks for Clint Eastwood movies; we're talking about Western civilization. That means that for pretty much *any* genre of music you're likely to play—whether it's rock, pop, blues, jazz, or classical—this scale is the foundation. Something this important is definitely worth learning, so let's dig in!

> **TIP: THEORY ALERT!**
>
> This chapter has a lot of information; make sure to take things slowly enough that you can digest them. Because of the amount of material in this chapter, we'll spend more time on shapes and concepts and less time introducing major-scale licks for you to incorporate into your repertoire. By now, you've certainly been coming up with your *own* licks, and I encourage you to do that throughout this lesson. Whenever you need a break from learning a new shape or reading about theoretical concepts, just turn to the "Arkansas Traveler" jam track (track 85) in the middle of this lesson and practice playing the scale and coming up with your own licks.

MAJOR SCALE CONSTRUCTION

The major scale has seven different notes, and it's easy to visualize if you look at a piano keyboard: all the white keys from one C note to the next C note spell out a major scale. On your guitar, this is how it looks. (You can see I've included eight notes, instead of seven. The eighth note is actually the same as the first note—the *root*—an octave higher. A full scale sequence will usually include the root on the bottom and top; there still are only seven distinct notes, since one is duplicated.)

C MAJOR SCALE

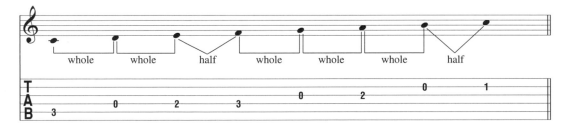

Compare this to the major pentatonic scale and you'll see that the extra two notes add quite a bit of character. Notice the "whole" and "half" markings between the tablature and notation. Those represent the distance (or interval, remember?) between each note. A *whole step* is two frets on one string of your guitar, and a *half step* is one fret. The beauty of this is that if you memorize this formula (whole–whole–half–whole–whole–whole–half), you can build *any* major scale. Let's try building a G major scale by starting on G:

G Major Scale

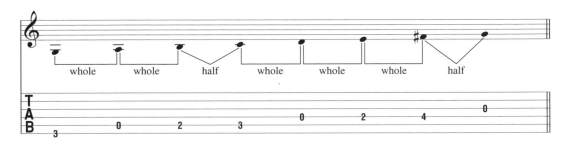

Now let's build an A major scale by starting on A:

A Major Scale

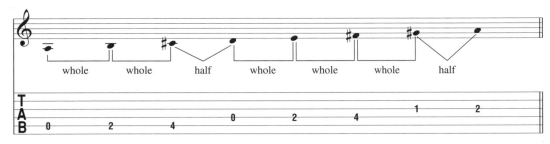

You can even build a scale all along one string. Here's how that A major scale looks if we keep going up the fifth string:

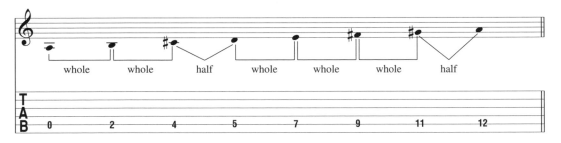

You've heard the major scale in innumerable songs. For instance, here's the melody from "The Battle Hymn of the Republic."

Track 83
00:00

And "When the Saints Go Marching In" is another good example:

TIP: KEY SIGNATURES

When you figure out the major scale for a note, any sharps or flats in that scale make up the *key signature* for that key. For instance, the A major scale has three sharps—F♯, C♯, and G♯—so the key signature for A major is three sharps (specifically, those three sharps). To keep things less cluttered with sharps written on every note, the key signature is written at the very beginning of each staff, directly after the clef. With this key signature established on each staff of music, you don't need to write out every sharp or flat:

MAJOR SCALE SHAPES

Just like all the other scales we've learned, there are plenty of major scale patterns. We'll go back to the C major scale, and here's Pattern 1, which corresponds to the same place on the neck as major pentatonic Pattern 1. (Remember, the notes from the major pentatonic scale are taken from the major scale.) The root note is the second note in this pattern:

C MAJOR SCALE PATTERN 1

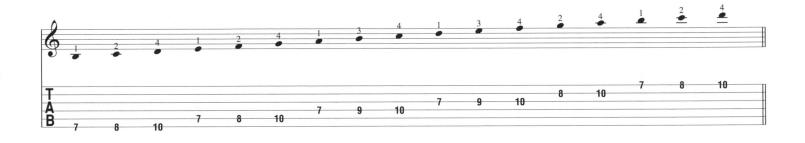

Since there are seven notes, we can actually play *seven* different major scale patterns (instead of the five for major pentatonic). Here are the other six shapes:

C Major Scale Pattern 2

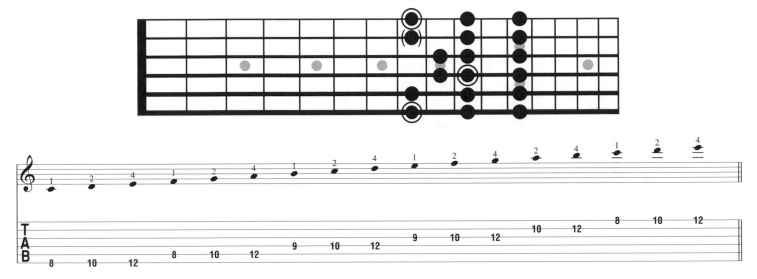

C Major Scale Pattern 3

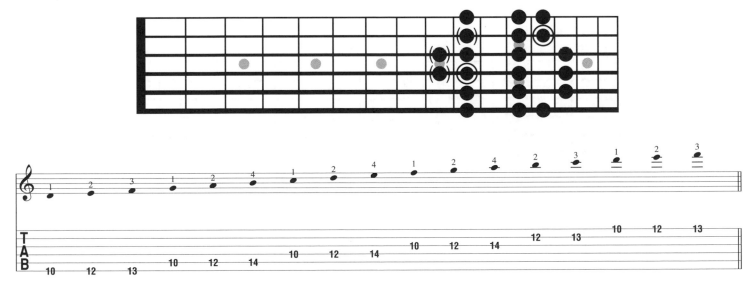

C Major Scale Pattern 4

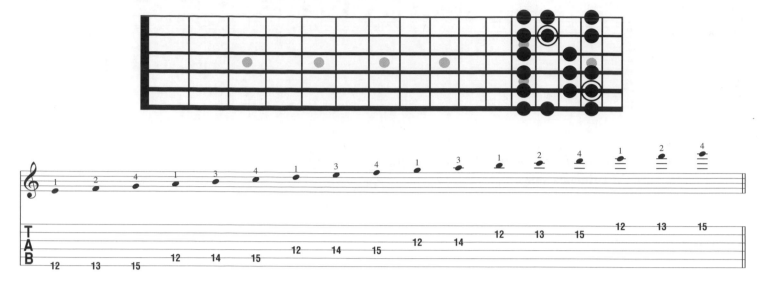

C Major Scale Pattern 5

C Major Scale Pattern 6

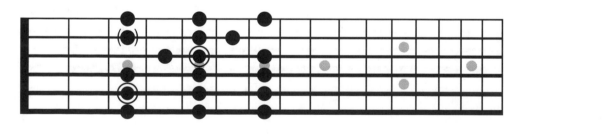

C Major Scale Pattern 7

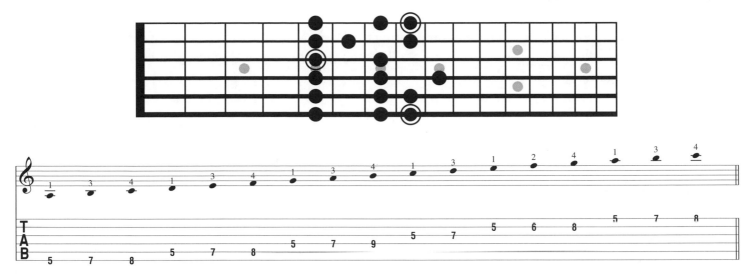

Notice how some of the patterns require more stretching than the pentatonic patterns. With more notes, some of them don't fall as easily under the fingers. But with a little extra practice, your fingers shouldn't have too much trouble making those stretches, even at high speeds. Also note how several of the fretboard diagrams show extra notes in parentheses that are not included in the notation and tablature versions below. These are alternate fingerings for the last note on the previous string, and you can use them instead of the note on the lower string if you like (though they'll occasionally put your fingers between two positions). Before you try the alternate fingerings, first make sure you're comfortable playing the scales as they appear in the notation and tablature.

TIP: MOVING BETWEEN PATTERNS

You can move between major scale patterns just like you did with the pentatonic scales, by either 1) sliding from position to position, or by 2) spreading your fingers so that you play the three notes of one pattern with your first three fingers and play the next scale note *on the same string* with your pinky (which will put you into position for the next pattern). Practice moving between patterns in this manner as much as you can, and the smoother you get at it, the more you'll be able to effortlessly move around the fretboard.

To help you get started, here's a diagram of all of the notes of a C major scale from the nut up to the twelfth fret.

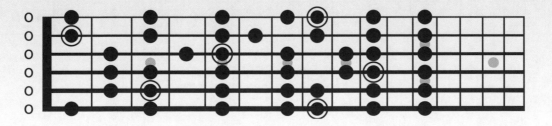

ARKANSAS TRAVELER

Now let's try out the major scale in a song. This time, rather than kick out a solo, we'll play the traditional tune "Arkansas Traveler," which makes great use of the major scale. This song is in the key of D major (notice the key signature of two sharps at the beginning of the song).

ARKANSAS TRAVELER

Track 84

Southern American Folksong
Copyright © 2010 by HAL LEONARD CORPORATION
International Copyright Secured   All Rights Reserved

Pay close attention to the fingerings, which have your index, middle, ring, and pinky fingers assigned to the second, third, fourth, and fifth frets, respectively. (We're playing at the nut with open strings, so we're not adhering to any of the moveable patterns.) Note that, while your index finger is positioned up at the second fret for the whole song, you can still play the open E string—allowing you to access more frets than you can up the neck.

Now it's your turn to play with the major scale and experiment with all of the moveable major scale patterns we've learned. Our jam track uses the chord progression from "Arkansas Traveler." Play the melody for "Arkansas Traveler," modify the melodies, or come up with your own licks and riffs.

ARKANSAS TRAVELER JAM TRACK

Track 85

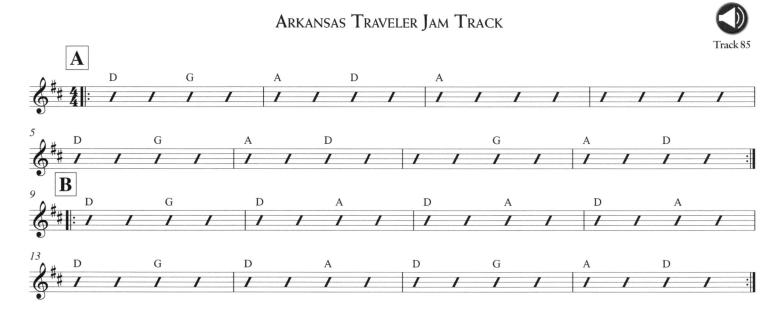

CHORD FUNCTIONS

Have you ever heard someone say "just go to the *five* chord," or something similar, and wondered what they were talking about? Well, the major scale can unlock the answer for you. Better yet, when you're armed with this knowledge, you'll be able to analyze major-key songs and understand them better, plus you'll be able to lead others by calling out chord progressions. It will also help you follow other musicians more easily, too.

Here's how it works: you can build chords from each note of the major scale by stacking two 3rds on top of each note. This may sound complicated, but it's not. A *3rd* is two notes away from any another note in the scale. So, that means that in an A major scale, C♯ is a 3rd away from A, and E is a 3rd away from C♯. Some 3rds are three frets apart, and those are called *minor 3rds*, whereas some 3rds are four frets apart, and those are called *major 3rds*. If you build these three-note chords (also called *triads*) along an A major scale, these are the chords you get:

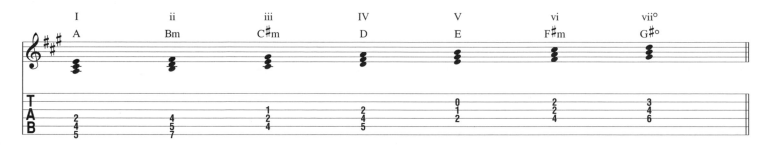

This process of building chords from each note of a scale is known as *harmonizing a scale*. Now that we know what chords we have in the key of A, we'll use Roman numerals to label our "chord functions," with uppercase denoting a major chord and lowercase denoting a minor chord (*see previous example*). The *chord functions* are essentially the way that they relate to each other in a key. In the key of A, we can see that an A chord is the "I" chord, a Bm chord is the "ii" chord, and so on.

> ### TIP: THESE CHORDS SHAPES ARE FOR ANALYZING—NOT FOR PLAYING
>
> I've included tablature in the chord-function example, and you may notice that these are pretty funky versions of each chord. These are root-position triad voicings that you may play on the piano, but rarely do you actually play chords this way on the guitar; instead, this is just the process you need to go through to figure out which chords to play in any key and what chord functions as what number in any key. Once you have it figured out, you can play a standard root-position or barre chord for those chords.

You may have heard of a "I–IV–V" progression before; it's one of the most common progressions around. Check out the chords on the previous page, looking at the Roman numerals, and you'll see that a I–IV–V progression in the key of A is actually an A–D–E chord progression. That's just like the progression from "Twist and Shout" and many, many other songs. Let's take a little playing diversion to fire up that progression as a backing track, and you can practice some A major scales and solos over the chord progression:

Track 86
00:00

Before we go further, there's one little wrinkle in our major scale chord functions. Look back at the example with the stacked chords and you'll notice that the seventh degree has a G♯ *diminished* chord. While this is a great chord, it's not that common in popular guitar music. Instead, the ♭VII chord is often substituted in here. The only difference between the ♭7th and this diminished chord is that the ♭VII chord has a G♮ as its lowest note, instead of a G♯; in this case, the ♭VII chord would be a G major chord:

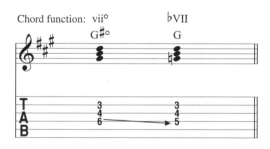

Songs like "Sweet Home Alabama" use the ♭VII chord in the classic I–♭VII–IV chord progression:

Track 86
00:12

SECTION IV: Lead

Now for the fun part! These chord relationships are the same for *every* major key. Let's figure out what a I–IV–V progression in the key of G looks like. First, we'll build a G major scale:

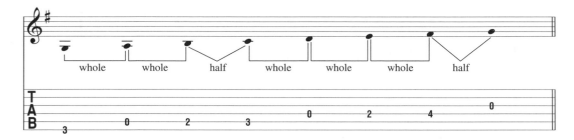

Now let's build our chord functions along the G major scale:

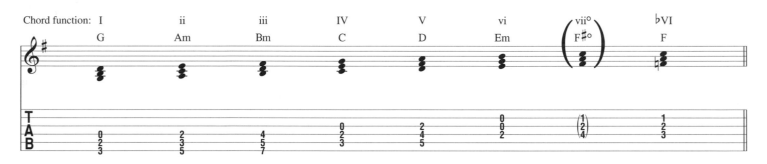

Looking at what we've built, we can see that a I–IV–V chord progression in the key of G is a G–C–D chord progression:

Track 86
00:25

Let's do one more before moving on. A classic progression in pop and jazz is the I–vi–ii–V progression (remember that those lowercase Roman numerals mean that those chords are minor chords). We'll try that progression in the key of D, so first we'll build a D major scale:

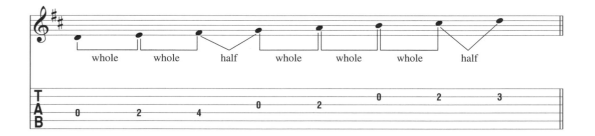

Now we'll build the chord functions for the D major scale:

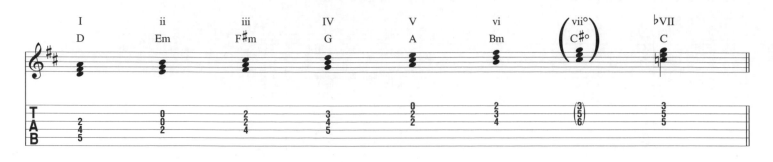

And now we can see that a I–vi–ii–V chord progression in D is D–Bm–Em–A:

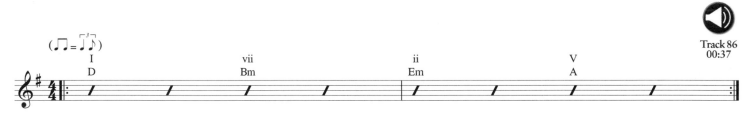

Track 86
00:37

This may seem like a laborious process, but once you learn your major scales inside and out and work with chord functions enough, you'll have all this information handy in your memory banks and won't have to figure it out every time.

146   SECTION IV: Lead

CHAPTER 20: THE MINOR SCALE

When you look at important scales, the *minor scale* is right up there with the major scale. With these two scales under your belt, you can solo over the majority of songs out there. On top of that, when you understand how these two scales work and relate to each other, you're well on your way towards understanding the foundations of theory behind Western music.

> **TIP: THEORY ALERT!**
>
> This chapter has a lot of information (just like **Chapter 19**), so don't rush through it. The extra information means we'll spend more time on shapes and concepts and less time with licks. Whenever you need a break from a new shape or theoretical concept, turn to the "Carolan's Dream" jam track (track 88) in the middle of this lesson and practice the minor scale shapes you've learned while coming up with your own licks.

MINOR SCALE CONSTRUCTION

People often say that the major scale sounds "happy," and that the minor scale sounds "sad." It's the order of intervals in these scales that give them their unique sounds (remember: an interval is the distance between two notes; in this case the intervals are whole steps and half steps). Like the major scale, the minor scale has seven notes. But the whole steps and half steps between those notes show up in a different order:

A MINOR SCALE

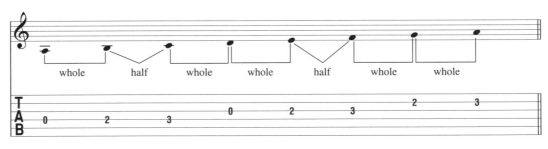

A MAJOR SCALE

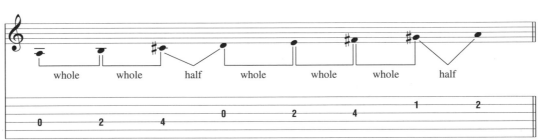

As you can see, the minor scale's 3rd, 6th, and 7th degrees are all one half step lower than those of the major scale, making the minor scale formula: whole–half–whole–whole–half–whole–whole. Using this formula, let's build a G minor scale:

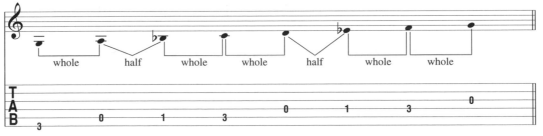

You can build a minor scale on any note by following this formula.

You'll hear the minor scale in many songs. One such example is the melody to "Joshua Fought the Battle of Jericho."

Track 87

"House of the Rising Sun" (from **Chapter 9**) is another good example of a minor-scale melody.

RELATIVE MINOR AND MAJOR SCALES

Now let's take a look at the relationship between major and minor scales. To show you how closely related they are, let's look at an A minor scale and a C major scale:

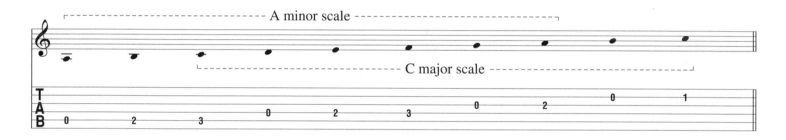

As you can see, they have exactly the same notes! An A minor scale is essentially a C major scale that starts and ends on A. These two scales are relative to each other—the A minor is the *relative minor* to C major, and C major is the *relative major* to A minor. (We touched on this concept with pentatonic scales.) Relative major and minor scales always share this exact relationship: the relative major scale starts on the 3rd degree (note) of any minor scale, and the relative minor scale starts on the 6th degree of any major scale.

Now let's build a D minor scale and figure out what scale is its relative major:

D Minor Scale

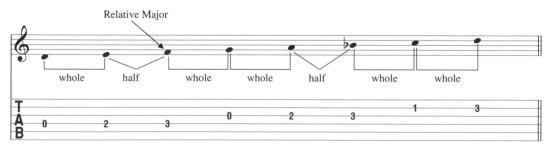

If you look at the 3rd degree, you can see that F major is the relative major of D minor. Sure enough, they have exactly the same notes:

F Major Scale

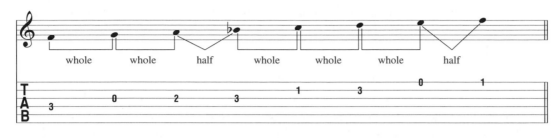

Let's try one going the other way. Let's find out what the relative minor scale of G major is:

G Major Scale

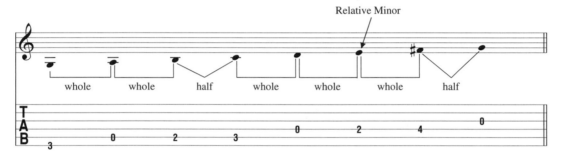

The 6th degree is E, so an E minor scale is the relative minor of G major. Let's check by building the E minor scale. Sure enough, it has exactly the same notes as G major:

E Minor Scale

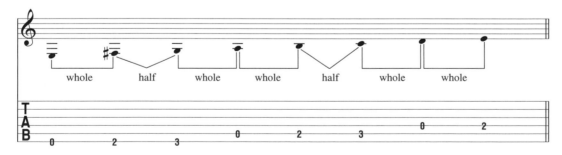

MINOR SCALE SHAPES

Since we know that the minor scale shares the same notes as the major scale—but starts in a different place—it makes sense that all of the minor scale shapes will share the same patterns as those for the major scale. They'll just start in different places. All of these patterns should seem familiar, but notice how the root notes are in different places:

A MINOR SCALE PATTERN 1

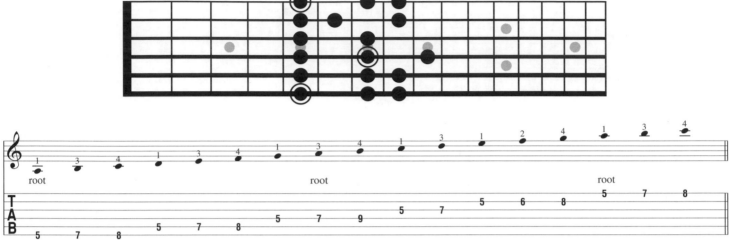

Since there are seven notes, we can actually play *seven* different minor scale patterns (instead of the five for minor pentatonic). Here are the other six shapes:

A MINOR SCALE PATTERN 2

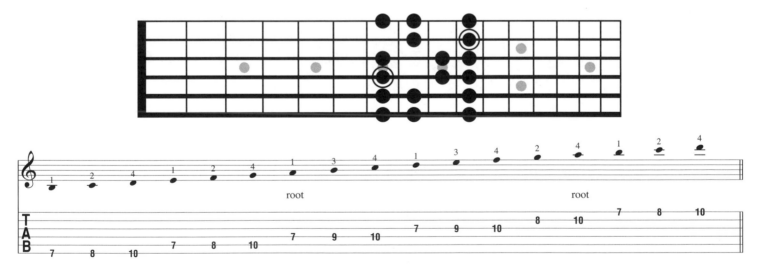

SECTION IV: Lead

A Minor Scale Pattern 3

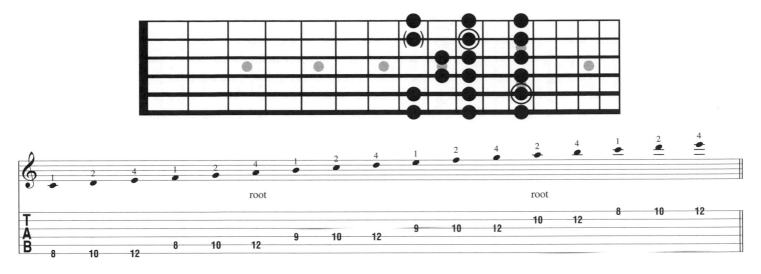

A Minor Scale Pattern 4

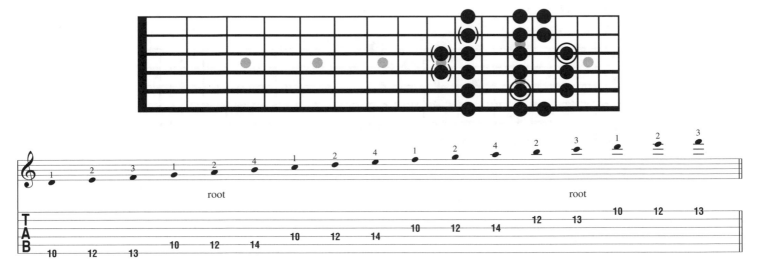

A Minor Scale Pattern 5

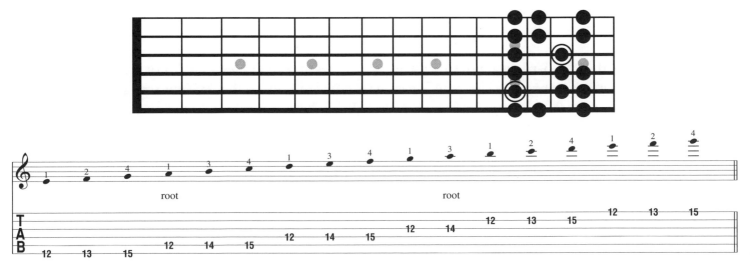

A Minor Scale Pattern 6

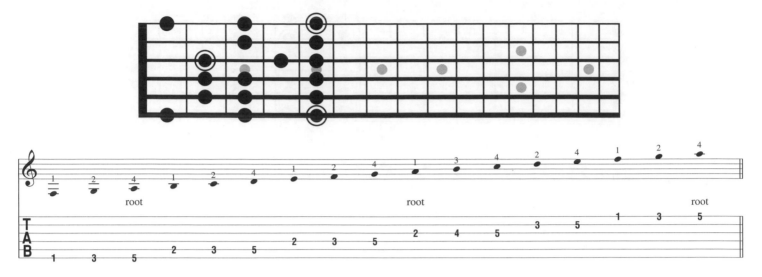

A Minor Scale Pattern 7

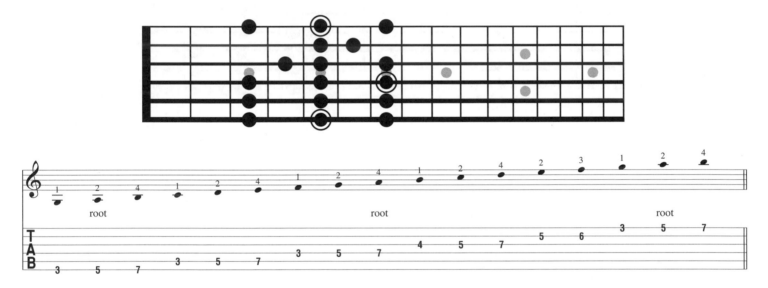

Notice how a few of the fretboard diagrams show some extra notes in parentheses that are not included in the notation and tablature patterns. These are alternate fingerings for the last note on the previous string, and you can use them instead of the note on the lower string, if you like (though they'll occasionally put your fingers between two positions). Before you try the alternate fingerings, first make sure you're comfortable playing the scales as they appear in the notation and tablature.

You can move between minor scale patterns just like you did with the pentatonic scales, by either 1) sliding from position to position, or by 2) spreading your fingers so that you play the three notes of one pattern with your first three fingers and play the next scale note *on the same string* with your pinky (which will put you into position for the next pattern). Practice moving between patterns in this manner as much as you can, and the smoother you get at it, the more you'll be able to effortlessly move around the fretboard and see how it all fits together.

To help you get started, here's a diagram of all of the notes of a *C minor* scale from the nut up to the twelfth fret.

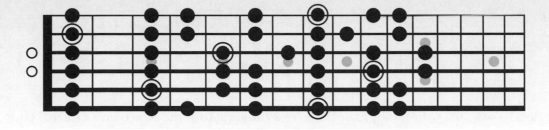

CAROLAN'S DREAM (MOLLY McALPIN)

Let's practice the minor scale by playing "Carolan's Dream." While this song is often credited to Irish harpist and composer Turlough O'Carolan, his version was modeled after Thomas Connellan's tune "Molly McAlpin," and you'll find the song under both names. There are quite a few chord changes here, though I've tried to keep the chord changes to a minimum (some arrangements change chords even quicker than this!). For the most part, we're playing in open position with a few stretches up to the fifth fret, but notice how we briefly move up to Pattern 1 in measures 12–14, and notice how the use of open strings during our position shifts allows us a little extra time to move our hand from position to position.

CAROLAN'S DREAM

Track 88

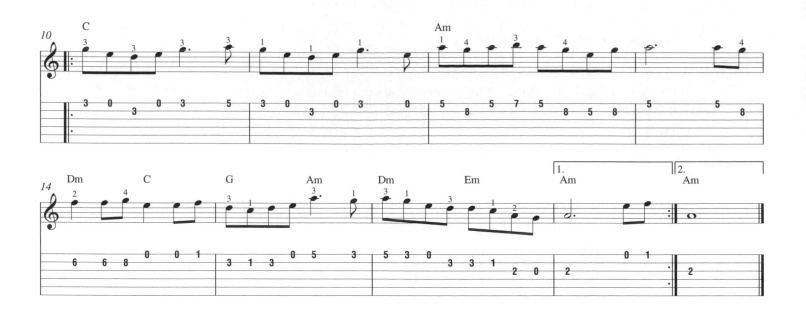

Now it's your turn to practice your minor scale patterns by soloing over the "Carolan's Dream" chord progression.

CAROLAN'S DREAM JAM TRACK

Track 89

MINOR-KEY CHORD FUNCTIONS

Now let's take a look at minor-key chord functions. (For a refresher on chord functions, see **Chapter 19**). As we did with the major scale, we'll build chords on each scale degree to find what chords go with the A minor scale.

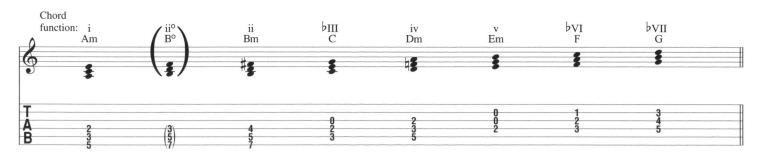

Looking at the Roman numerals, we can see that the chord functions for minor keys are i, ii, ♭III, iv, v, ♭VI, and ♭VII. (Notice how a minor chord is used instead of a diminished chord for the second degree).

> ## TIP: CHORD FUNCTION SHORTCUT
>
> Once you know the chord functions for minor and major keys, they will always have the same relationship, no matter what key you're in. Once you know your scales by memory, this means you won't have to build every scale and map out its chord functions to figure out a progression in a key. For instance, if you need to play a i–iv–v chord progression in the key of G minor, you'll know that the 4th and 5th scale degrees in a G minor scale are C and D, respectively; you'll also know that these chord are minor chords in a minor key. Without having to spend much time at all, you'll know that the progression is Gm–Cm–Dm.

One common minor chord progression in the classic-rock realm is the i–♭VII–♭VI, heard in "Stairway to Heaven" or "All Along the Watchtower." Let's try out that progression in the key of A minor:

Track 90
00:00

Now let's practice our new chord-function knowledge by figuring out this progression in another key: E minor. First, let's build an E minor scale:

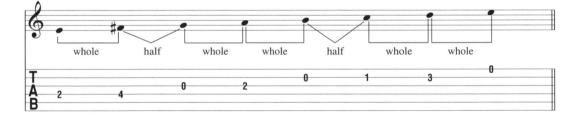

Next, we'll harmonize the scale:

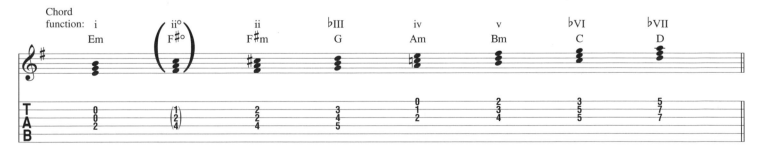

Now we see that a I–♭VII–♭VI chord progression in the key of E minor is Em–D–C:

> **TIP**: Blues Chord Functions
>
> Now that you know about chord functions, we can look at the functions for a blues so that you can play the blues in any key. The basic progression for a 12-bar blues is I (four measures)–IV (two measures)–I (two measures)–V (one measure)–IV (one measure)–I (two measures). So, without showing the number of measures per chord, that's I–IV–I–V–IV–I.
>
> For minor key blues songs, just substitute the minor functions in for our chords: i (four measures)–iv (two measures)–i (two measures)–v (one measure)–iv (one measure) –i (two measures).
>
> Remember that you can always throw in a V (or v) in the final measure! If you continue exploring the blues, you'll discover there are limitless variations on this progression, but this basic format should help you follow most of the blues progressions you'll encounter.

SECTION IV: Lead

CHAPTER 21: MIXING MAJOR AND MINOR PENTATONIC SCALES

Though most blues and rock players spend a lot of time in the major and minor pentatonic scales, some of their best solos can't be recreated with just one of those scales. When you slide *between* the two scales—and even mix them completely together—you can coax a whole new world of sounds from your guitar that ride the fence between a major and minor tonality. It's techniques like these that help players take their soloing to a new level.

SLIDING PATTERNS TO SWITCH SCALES

The easiest way to mix minor and major pentatonic scales together is by sliding patterns back and forth on the fretboard. Since we already know that the minor and major pentatonic scales share the same shapes, all we have to do is determine which ones match each other. For instance, Pattern 5 of the A major pentatonic scale is exactly the same shape as Pattern 1 of the A minor pentatonic scale:

A MAJOR PENTATONIC PATTERN 5

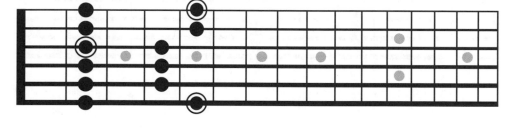

A MINOR PENTATONIC PATTERN 1

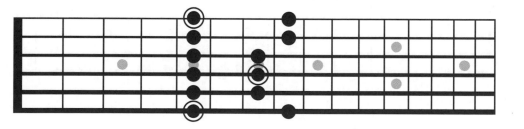

So we can mix the two together in our licks by sliding between the two, like this (up three frets from major to minor pentatonic and down three frets from minor to major pentatonic):

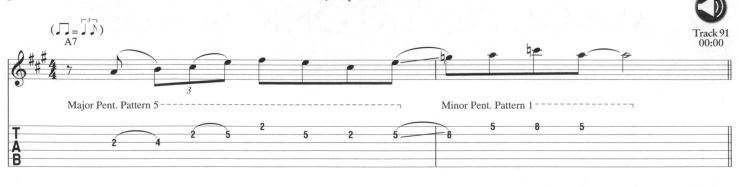

For another example, the Pattern 1 major pentatonic and Pattern 2 minor pentatonic scales share the same shape:

A Major Pentatonic Pattern 1

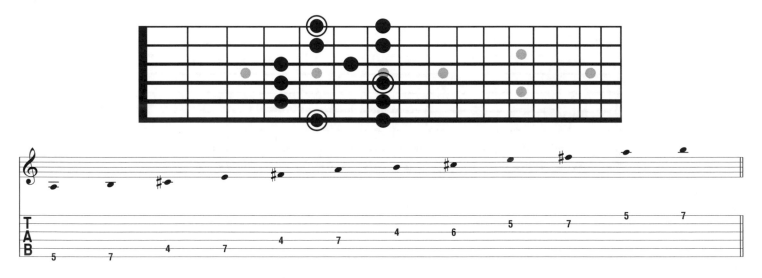

A Minor Pentatonic Pattern 2

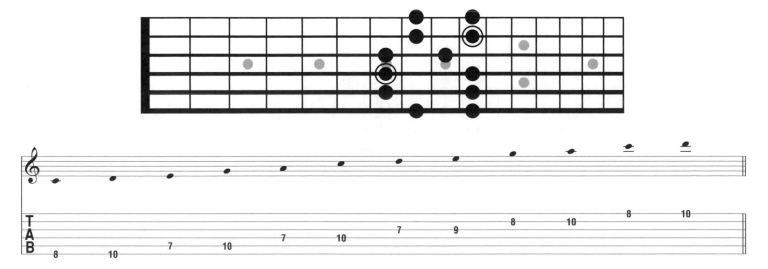

SECTION IV: Lead

Again, we can slide three frets to mix these sounds together (up three frets from major to minor pentatonic, and down three frets from minor to major pentatonic).

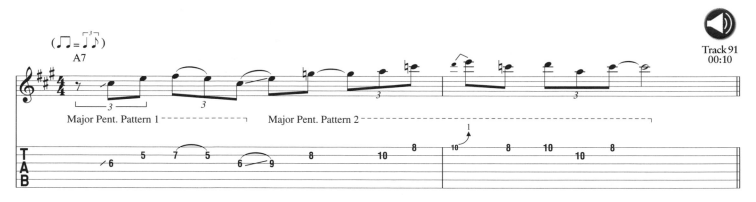

Track 91
00:10

TIP: SLIDE THREE FRETS FROM ANY SHAPE

Essentially, whatever shape you're in, you can slide three frets to play out of the other scale type: for minor pentatonic, shift down three frets to reach its major pentatonic counterpart; for major pentatonic, shift up three frets to reach its minor pentatonic counterpart.

SWITCHING SCALES IN THE SAME POSITION

The next way we can mix these scales together is by switching between patterns in the same position. For instance, both major and minor pentatonic Pattern 1 scales are in the same area. For A minor and major pentatonic, that would be here:

A MAJOR PENTATONIC PATTERN 1

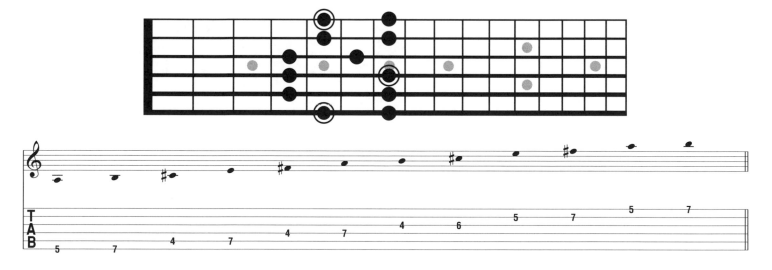

A Minor Pentatonic Pattern 1

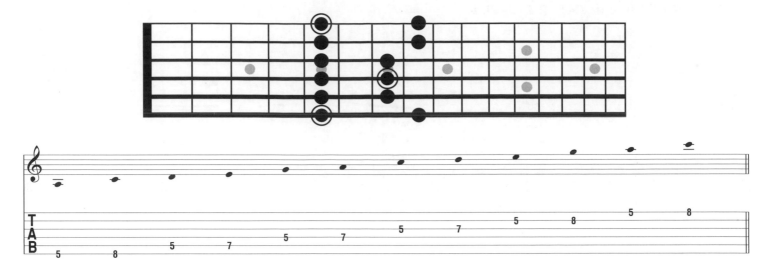

So, you could move between these patterns within a lick, like this phrase, which works well over an A7–D7 chord change:

Track 91
00:19

Here's another example, using Pattern 5 shapes (if you need to review these shapes, go back to **Chapters 15** and **16**):

Track 91
00:29

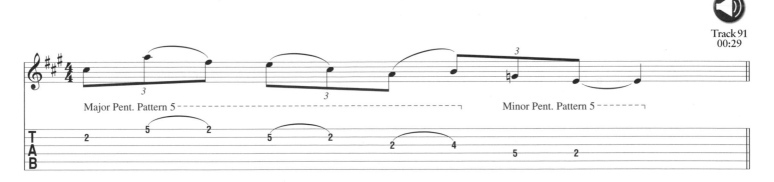

BLENDING SCALES

To seamlessly blend the sounds together, let's look at what happens when we literally put the two scales together:

Mixed A Minor and Major Pentatonic Scales

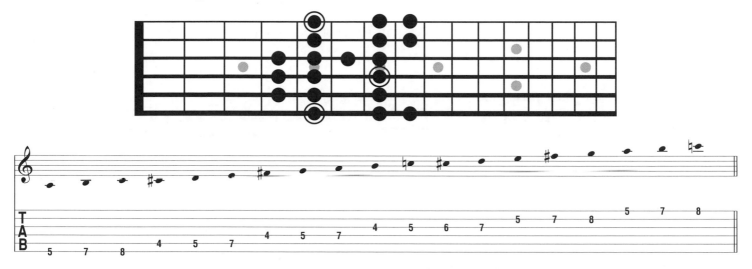

This pattern may look intimidating and difficult to play. But the point isn't necessarily to run this pattern up and down—it's to see how these blended scales fit together. Once you can visualize that, you can pick and choose the notes to use and grab them in the ways that make the most sense for any individual lick or melodic line. Notice how this super-scale includes *three* half steps in a row (2nd–♭3rd–3rd–4th)! This allows for some cool and slinky lines, and you don't have to play the whole scale up and down to get them. For instance, check out this great move that highlights double stops and a move from the ♭3rd to the major 3rd, which is a staple in blues soloing:

Track 92
00:00

Here's another lick that plays off of the mixed 3rds. The blended notes of these scales can skirt both major and minor sounds, creating interesting tensions against the background chords:

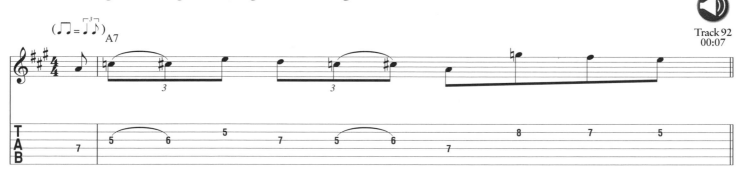

Track 92
00:07

> ### TIP: Blend Other Minor and Major Pentatonic Patterns
>
> You can combine any set of major and minor pentatonic patterns. Since you've learned all of the major and minor pentatonic patterns in *Chapters 15* and *16*, go through and combine them yourself. Then construct your own licks and see which licks fall more easily into each mixed pattern.

BLENDED MINOR AND MAJOR PENTATONIC SOLO

Now let's try our new tricks out in a solo. The following solo uses all three of the techniques in this chapter: sliding between shared minor and major pentatonic shapes, moving between patterns in the same position, and blending the scales into complete phrases.

MINOR AND MAJOR PENTATONIC SOLO

Track 93

Now it's your turn to try out your own licks over the jam track. Note that the jam track cycles through the first eight measures four times so you can practice your licks a bit longer. That two-measure tag from the solo then shows up at the very end:

MINOR AND MAJOR PENTATONIC JAM TRACK

Track 94

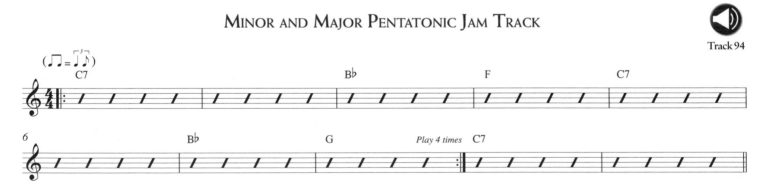

CHAPTER 22: OPEN-STRING LEADS

When you play acoustic guitar—especially in an unamplified setting—your guitar can get lost in the mix of other instruments and voices. Perhaps your rhythm guitarist gets excited and starts hacking away at full volume on all six strings. If that's the case, there's *no way* you're going to project your single-note lead lines and licks over the top! Aside from using heavy strings and picks, digging in extra hard, and playing huge-sounding dreadnought guitars, another way you can help cut through the mix is to play *open-string leads*. Any time you add an open string to your single-note lines, you'll increase the volume. But those open strings also resonate and sustain much longer than fretted notes, so you'll also be adding sustain to your licks and melodies, and this is a great thing in an unamplified setting, where the sound can get swallowed up by the audience, carpeting, and background chatter.

OPEN-STRING CHORD TONES

We'll start by using an open string in situations where it functions as a *chord tone* of the background chords. For instance, the chord tones of an E chord are E, G#, and B, so if we're playing over an E chord, we'd make sure to use an open string that is one of those notes.

LEADS WITH THE OPEN E STRING

In the key of E major, the I chord is E, and the notes of an E chord are E, G#, and B. So, we can use the high E string against an E chord progression, since it's the root note of E chord. Now if we want to solo using an E major scale, we'll build that on the B string and play the scale against that open E string, like this:

E Major Scale with Open E String

We're playing along the B string because it's a bit more difficult (though certainly doable) to play notes on the other strings along with the open E string. Once you're comfortable with this, you can construct lead lines, like this, over an E chord:

Track 95
00:00

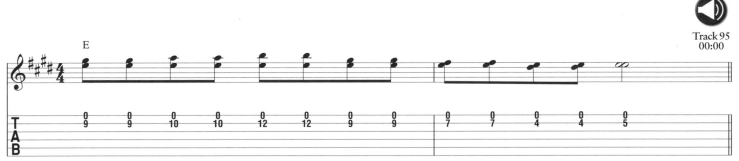

Notice how the technique really adds to this lick over an E chord progression.

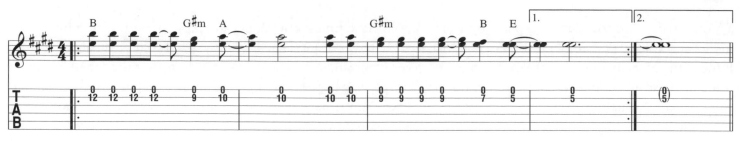

Notice how the previous chord progression had more than just an E chord in the background and not all of these chords have an E note as a chord tone. We're not going to worry about changing that open string every time the rhythm part changes chords. Instead, we'll look at the defining chord of a progression and match that chord only—the "I" chord in a key, if you're talking about chord functions. If we match a note in a key's I chord, all the other chords in that key will generally sound fine with the same open string. (For more on chord theory, see the **Appendix**).

You can also use that open E string over chord progressions in A, since the E note is part of an A chord (the notes A–C#–E), and A is the I chord in the key of A. In this case, we'll use an A major scale for our melodies:

A MAJOR SCALE WITH OPEN E STRING

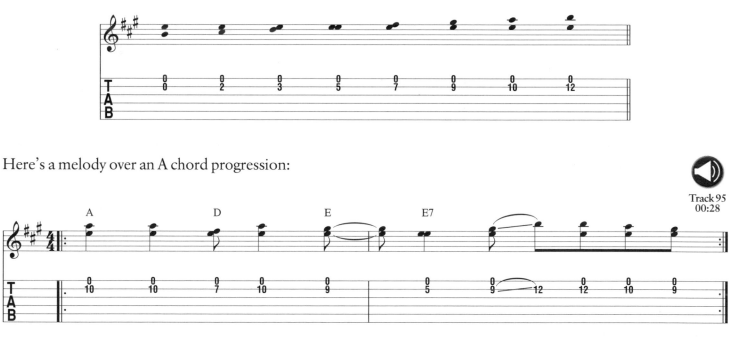

Here's a melody over an A chord progression:

Our E note also fits into a C chord, which has the notes C, E, and G. In C, let's use the C major scale, so let's first familiarize ourselves with that scale on the second string against the open first string:

C MAJOR SCALE WITH OPEN E STRING

And let's try out a lick in C:

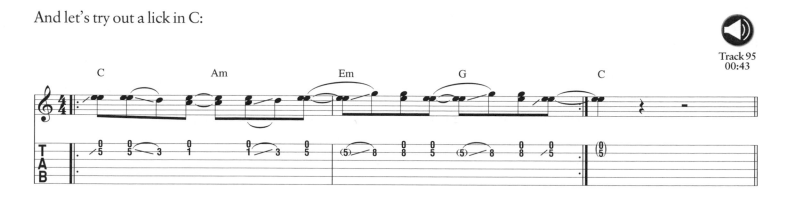

And don't forget about minor keys. That high E note is the minor third of a C#m chord, so we could play it over a C#m progression. In this case, we'd probably play out of the C# minor scale, so let's play that against the open E string to get familiar with it:

C# MINOR SCALE WITH OPEN E STRING

Here's a melody carved out over a C#m–A–E–B chord progression:

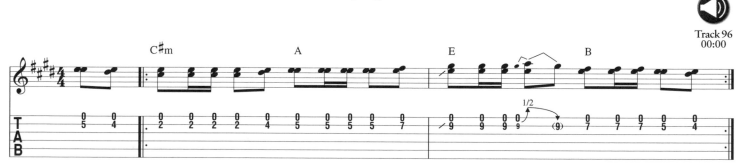

LEADS WITH THE OPEN B STRING

Now let's try the open B string for leads. In this case, it's easiest to play melodies *above* that note—on the high E string. We know B is part of an E chord (which has the notes E, G#, and B), so let's try an E chord progression again. This time we'll work out of an E major scale on the top string:

E MAJOR SCALE WITH OPEN B STRING

Pulling off to the open string is a cool effect that's easier to manage on the highest string, so let's try a lick with a few pull-offs.

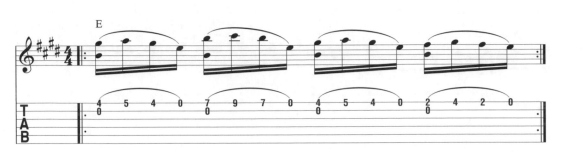

Track 96
00:20

With the B string, you can also play leads on the third string. And also remember: you don't always have to use the major (or minor) scale, like we have earlier in this lesson. Let's try one on the third string using an E minor pentatonic scale. First, here's that E minor pentatonic scale across the third string, coupled with the open second string:

E MINOR PENTATONIC SCALE ON THIRD STRING WITH OPEN B STRING

And here's an E minor pentatonic melody to try out on these strings:

Track 96
00:31

So far, we've played licks in E against both the open E and B strings, but if you put those two together, you've got a longer scale to solo with and you don't have to move up and down one string as much. Here's an example of how you might do that by playing a lick in E major on the top three strings that uses the open E and B strings in different places:

Track 96
00:47

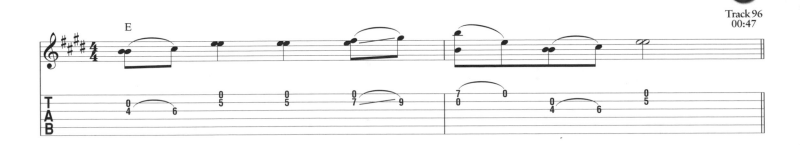

OPEN STRINGS AS NON-CHORD TONES

So far, we've used open strings when they fit perfectly into the background chords. But an open string doesn't have to be a chord tone of the underlying chords to sound good. Let's go back to the open E string and play it with a D major scale on the second string:

D Major Scale with Open E String

It actually sounds pretty good. That E note is actually the 9th of a D chord, and when you play it over a D scale, it adds a Dadd9 sound, like the following chord:

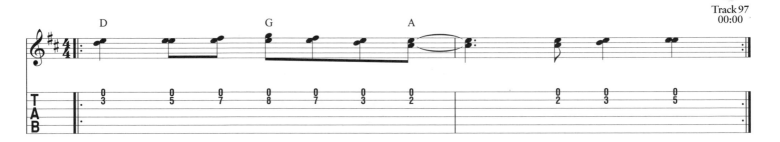

Let's try a D melody now using the open E string and see how that sounds:

Track 97
00:00

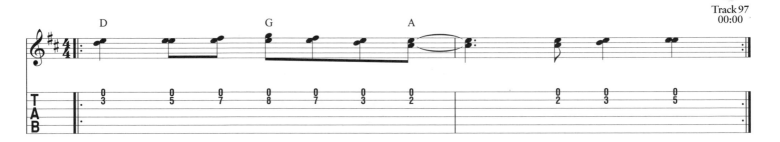

There are actually many different chords and progressions that you can work this technique into. Try some out yourself; just experiment by trial and error or by thinking about which notes will sound good with certain chords. Let's try another. Since an E note is the major 7th of an Fmaj7 chord, it enhances that major 7th sound if we play an F major scale against the open E string (for more on chord theory, see the **Appendix**).

F Major Scale with Open E String

Licks built from this scale and open string will sound great over chord progressions with an Fmaj7 chord, or will make regular F chords *sound* like they're Fmaj7 chords. Here's one melody to get you going:

Track 97
00:15

See what other chord progressions and keys you can find that work well with the open E or B string as a backdrop.

TIP: USE YOUR CAPO

If you want to use this technique but you're having trouble finding something that works on a certain chord progression, try using your capo. For instance, if you're playing over a song in B♭ and you want to use that open E string, it will sound terrible against a B♭ chord—the E rubs up against the F note in a B♭ since it is so close. But if you put a capo on the first fret, your highest open string will now be an F, which *is* a chord tone of B♭.

LEADS WITH TWO OPEN STRINGS

So far we've looked at lead lines and melodies that play against the open B or E strings. You could try a lower string on your own, but the lower strings tend to be less effective for this technique for two reasons: 1) when you drone the low strings, things tend to get muddy; and 2) the bass of the low strings doesn't cut through the mix nearly as well as the treble of the higher strings. But one other thing we can look at is using *multiple* open strings along with a lead line. Let's try an E scale on the third string against the top two strings:

E MAJOR SCALE WITH OPEN B AND E STRING

Playing a lick with three strings adds quite a bit of volume:

Track 97
00:29

Let's try out another unique one by playing an A major scale with the top two strings. This one creates an Aadd9 sound (similar to the open E string creating a Dadd9 sound with a D scale):

A MAJOR SCALE WITH OPEN B AND E STRINGS

Here's a lick with that Aadd9 sound. Try it out and come up with some of your own:

Track 97
00:39

OPEN STRING SOLO

Now let's try a whole solo with this technique. While the following solo uses open strings throughout, you don't *always* have to use it for every note of a solo. Sometimes it works great as the solo's climax—to help bring that part out even more. The technique also works especially well on sculpted hooks for songs.

OPEN STRING SOLO

Track 98

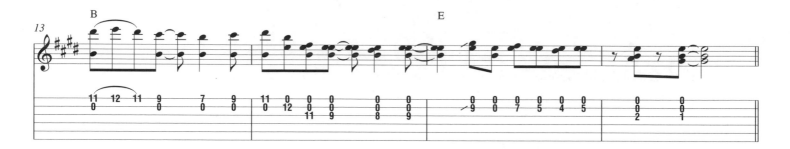

Now it's your turn! Here's the jam track from the previous solo. Let those open strings fly!

OPEN STRING JAM TRACK

Track 99

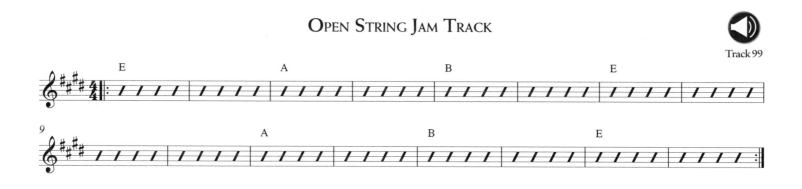

APPENDIX

CHORD THEORY

You don't need to know theory to play music, but it can help you understand the music you play better. If you'd like to learn more about chord-construction theory, read on!

TRIADS

Triad is a Greek word that means "three," and that's exactly what a triad contains—three notes! Triads are the most common type of chord. They are built by stacking two 3rds on top of each other. When we say "3rds," we're talking about intervals—the distance between notes. If you start on one note and move up the scale, the distance between the first note and the next note is a *2nd*. The distance between the first note and the third note is a *3rd*, between the first and fourth is a *4th*, and so on. A 3rd can be either major or minor, and stacking these 3rds on top of each other in different combinations creates four types of triads: major, minor, diminished, and augmented. Here is what's known as a C major triad:

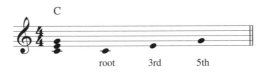

The defining note of a chord (its letter name) is called the *root*. Notice how the second note in the triad is the 3rd. The top note is called the 5th because its interval with the root is a 5th (count up yourself to see). After we take a closer look at intervals, we'll look at the different types of triads you can build with those intervals. So, continue on for more on triads.

INTERVALS

The *triad* section briefly discussed what an interval is: the distance between any two notes. Counting up from the first note to the second note will give you the interval between those two notes. That distance is quantified with a number, but intervals also have another component: their *quality*. The quality of any interval can be major, minor, diminished, augmented, or perfect. Looking at the twelve notes in a chromatic scale, along with their intervals, can help explain the differences between these qualities:

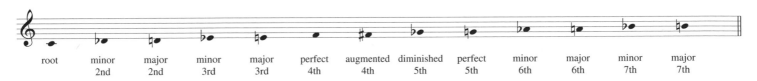

You may notice that every minor interval is one half step smaller than its major interval counterpart. The only intervals that are not major or minor are the *perfect* intervals—the 4th and 5th. Lowering a perfect interval (like the 4th) results in a diminished interval, while raising a perfect interval (like the 5th) results in an augmented interval. All the other non-perfect intervals can be diminished or augmented as well, though it rarely happens. Here's how: if you lower a minor interval by one-half step, it becomes diminished; and if you raise a major interval by one-half step, it becomes augmented.

Now let's look at all the different types of triads we can build with these intervals. There are four types: major, minor, diminished, and augmented. *Major triads* have a major 3rd and a perfect 5th, *minor triads* have a minor third and a perfect 5th, *diminished triads* have a minor third and a diminished fifth, and *augmented triads* have a major third and an augmented fifth:

Major triads are labeled with just a letter (C, above), minor triads are labeled with a lowercase "m" (Cm, above), diminished triads are labeled with a "°" (C), and augmented chords are labeled with a "+" (C+).

7TH CHORDS

Seventh chords are four-note chords that stack a 7th interval on top of a triad. There are six types of unaltered 7th chords: *dominant seventh* (labeled with a "7" after the chord's letter name), *minor seventh* (m7), *major seventh* (maj7), *minor major seventh* [m(maj7)], *minor seven* ♭5 (m7♭5, also known as *half-diminished*), and *diminished seventh* (°7). Here are the 7th chords with a C root:

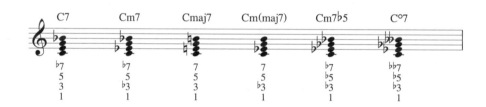

EXTENDED CHORDS

Beyond 7th chords, you can add further extensions to color the chord even more. Basically, you continue stacking 3rds on top of a 7th chord to build extended chords. Stack one 3rd on top and you have a 9th chord; add a 3rd to the 9th chord, and you have an 11th chord; and add a 3rd to that 11th chord to get a 13th chord.

Not all notes of an extended chord are necessary to complete the chord. This is especially true on guitar, where a full 13th chord would be impossible to play, since you'd need to play seven notes and you only have six strings! But some of the notes are more important to include than others. For a chord to be an extended chord, you have to include the 7th and the extension. After that, including the 3rd, root, and other extensions hold lesser priority. The least important note to include in an extended chord is the 5th.

It's also important to note that extensions can appear in a different octave than their numerical name implies. For instance, a 13th down one octave is a 6th. You can use that 6th (instead of a 13th) in your chord, and it will still be considered a 13th chord as long as you have a 7th in the chord, as well.

SUSPENDED, ADD, AND OTHER CHORDS

Suspended chords (sus) are formed when a note is substituted for a chord tone. In a sus4 chord, for instance, the 4th is substituted for the 3rd. *Add* chords are simply chords that add one or several notes to any particular chord. The difference between a sus4 and an add4 chord is that the sus4 does not include the 3rd, while the add4 does. Of course, like the English language, there are always a few exceptions. A triad with an added 6th is simply a 6th chord (though it could be written as an add6 chord), and a chord with the 6th and 9th added is simply called a "6/9 chord."

ALTERED CHORDS

Any chord can be altered, and that alteration is reflected in the chord's name. For instance, if you alter a 7th chord by lowering the 5th one half step, you have a $7^{\flat}5$ chord; raise the 5th of that 7th chord by one half step, and you have a $7^{\sharp}5$ chord.

INVERSIONS

Any time that the lowest note in a chord is not the root, the chord is in an *inversion*. The more notes you have in a chord, the more possible inversions you have. For instance, a 7th chord can be played in more inversions than a triad.

SAME SHAPES, DIFFERENT NAMES

Many chords can be called more than one name. For instance, a $^{\flat}5$th is equivalent to a $^{\sharp}11$, and a chord containing one of these notes could be labeled either way. Likewise, a $^{\sharp}5$th and a $^{\flat}13$th are also equivalent.

TIME SIGNATURES

Time signatures tell you what the rhythm is for a song and they appear at the beginning of a piece, just after the *key signature* (which is explained in the next section). Time signatures look like a fraction—with two numbers stacked on top of each other. The top number tells you how many beats there are in each measure, and the bottom number tells you what the note value for each beat is. To get the correct beat value for the bottom number, you have to pretend it's the bottom number of a fraction where the number "1" would be on top. For instance, the following time signature—4/4—indicates four beats per measure and that a quarter note (1/4) gets the beat.

Four-four time is the most common time signature, and you'll often see a "C" in place of the 4/4 marking; the "C" stands for "common time."

Waltzes, and many other three-beat songs, use a 3/4 time signature, which has three quarter-note beats per measure:

In 6/8 time, there are six beats per measure, and one *eighth note* gets the beat:

In 6/8 time, however, the beats are often grouped into two sets of three notes. In this case, though there *are* six beats per measure, it's often counted *one*-and-ah, *two*-and-ah, instead of *one*-two-three, *four*-five-six.

KEY SIGNATURES

Sharps and flats are referred to together as *accidentals*, and every key has its own set of accidentals that we call its *key signature*. The key signature is located at the beginning of a song and at the beginning of each new line of music. The following key signature has three sharps:

When *sharps* or *flats* appear in a key signature, every time a note is written on that line or space, you don't have to mark that it's a sharp or flat since that has been designated in the key signature. Because of this, key signatures make things easier to write. Of course, if there's a sharp in the key signature and you want the note to *not* be a sharped note, you have to put a *natural* (♮) in front of the note. If you want the note sharped again in the same measure, you have to write out that sharp to counteract the previous natural:

In the following measures, the key signature would apply again, and you wouldn't need to write out the sharp, though sometimes *courtesy accidentals* are added just to remind the performer of the key signature.

KEY SIGNATURES WITH FLATS

When flats occur in a key signature, they happen in the following order: B♭–E♭–A♭–D♭–G♭–C♭–F♭.

When your key signature has flats in it and you're playing in a *major* key, a quick way to know what key you are in is to look at the second-to-last flat. *That* is the key! For instance, when you have four flats (B♭, E♭, A♭, and D♭), the second-to-last flat is A♭, so you are in the key of A♭ major:

But what about when you have just one flat? If that's the case, you're in the key of F major:

When your key signature has flats and you're in a minor key, a quick way to know what key you're in is to count up two whole steps from the last flat, and that note is the key. For instance, when you have three flats, if you count up two whole steps from the last flat (A♭), you reach C; you're in the key of C minor:

If you have five flats, counting up two whole steps from the G♭, you reach B♭; you're in the key of B♭ minor.

KEY SIGNATURES WITH SHARPS

When sharps occur in a key signature, they appear in the following order: F♯–C♯–G♯–D♯–A♯–E♯–B♯. Notice how that's exactly *opposite* of the order that flats appear.

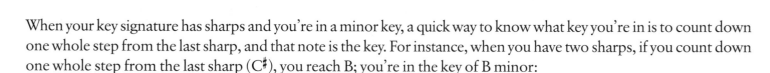

When your key signature has sharps in it and you're playing in a *major* key, a quick way to know what key you are in is to look at the last sharp, then move up one half step. For instance, when you have two sharps (F♯ and C♯), if you move up one half step from C♯, you reach D, which is the key:

When your key signature has sharps and you're in a minor key, a quick way to know what key you're in is to count down one whole step from the last sharp, and that note is the key. For instance, when you have two sharps, if you count down one whole step from the last sharp (C♯), you reach B; you're in the key of B minor:

If you have four sharps, counting down one whole step from the D♯, you reach C♯; you're in the key of C♯ minor.

Get Better at Guitar

...with these Great Guitar Instruction Books from Hal Leonard!

101 GUITAR TIPS
INCLUDES TAB

STUFF ALL THE PROS KNOW AND USE

by Adam St. James

This book contains invaluable guidance on everything from scales and music theory to truss rod adjustments, proper recording studio set-ups, and much more. The book also features snippets of advice from some of the most celebrated guitarists and producers in the music business, including B.B. King, Steve Vai, Joe Satriani, Warren Haynes, Laurence Juber, Pete Anderson, Tom Dowd and others, culled from the author's hundreds of interviews.

00695737 Book/Online Audio $16.99

AMAZING PHRASING
INCLUDES TAB

50 WAYS TO IMPROVE YOUR IMPROVISATIONAL SKILLS

by Tom Kolb

This book/audio pack explores all the main components necessary for crafting well-balanced rhythmic and melodic phrases. It also explains how these phrases are put together to form cohesive solos. Many styles are covered – rock, blues, jazz, fusion, country, Latin, funk and more – and all of the concepts are backed up with musical examples. The companion audio contains 89 demos for listening, and most tracks feature full-band backing.

00695583 Book/Online Audio $19.99

BLUES YOU CAN USE – 2ND EDITION

by John Ganapes

This comprehensive source for learning blues guitar is designed to develop both your lead and rhythm playing. Includes: 21 complete solos • blues chords, progressions and riffs • turnarounds • movable scales and soloing techniques • string bending • utilizing the entire fingerboard • and more. This second edition now includes audio and video access online!

00142420 Book/Online Media..................$19.99

FRETBOARD MASTERY
INCLUDES TAB

by Troy Stetina

Untangle the mysterious regions of the guitar fretboard and unlock your potential. *Fretboard Mastery* familiarizes you with all the shapes you need to know by applying them in real musical examples, thereby reinforcing and reaffirming your newfound knowledge. The result is a much higher level of comprehension and retention.

00695331 Book/Online Audio $19.99

FRETBOARD ROADMAPS – 2ND EDITION

ESSENTIAL GUITAR PATTERNS THAT ALL THE PROS KNOW AND USE

by Fred Sokolow

The updated edition of this bestseller features more songs, updated lessons, and a full audio CD! Learn to play lead and rhythm anywhere on the fretboard, in any key; play a variety of lead guitar styles; play chords and progressions anywhere on the fretboard; expand your chord vocabulary; and learn to think musically – the way the pros do.

00695941 Book/CD Pack..................$14.95

GUITAR AEROBICS
INCLUDES TAB

A 52-WEEK, ONE-LICK-PER-DAY WORKOUT PROGRAM FOR DEVELOPING, IMPROVING & MAINTAINING GUITAR TECHNIQUE

by Troy Nelson

From the former editor of *Guitar One* magazine, here is a daily dose of vitamins to keep your chops fine tuned! Musical styles include rock, blues, jazz, metal, country, and funk. Techniques taught include alternate picking, arpeggios, sweep picking, string skipping, legato, string bending, and rhythm guitar. These exercises will increase speed, and improve dexterity and pick- and fret-hand accuracy. The accompanying audio includes all 365 workout licks plus play-along grooves in every style at eight different metronome settings.

00695946 Book/Online Audio $19.99

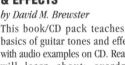

GUITAR CLUES
INCLUDES TAB

OPERATION PENTATONIC

by Greg Koch

Join renowned guitar master Greg Koch as he clues you in to a wide variety of fun and valuable pentatonic scale applications. Whether you're new to improvising or have been doing it for a while, this book/CD pack will provide loads of delicious licks and tricks that you can use right away, from volume swells and chicken pickin' to intervallic and chordal ideas. The CD includes 65 demo and play-along tracks.

00695827 Book/CD Pack..................$19.95

INTRODUCTION TO GUITAR TONE & EFFECTS

by David M. Brewster

This book/CD pack teaches the basics of guitar tones and effects, with audio examples on CD. Readers will learn about: overdrive, distortion and fuzz • using equalizers • modulation effects • reverb and delay • multi-effect processors • and more.

00695766 Book/CD Pack..................$14.99

PICTURE CHORD ENCYCLOPEDIA

This comprehensive guitar chord resource for all playing styles and levels features five voicings of 44 chord qualities for all twelve keys – 2,640 chords in all! For each, there is a clearly illustrated chord frame, as well as *an actual photo* of the chord being played! Includes info on basic fingering principles, open chords and barre chords, partial chords and broken-set forms, and more.

00695224..................$19.95

SCALE CHORD RELATIONSHIPS
INCLUDES TAB

by Michael Mueller & Jeff Schroedl

This book teaches players how to determine which scales to play with which chords, so guitarists will never have to fear chord changes again! This book/audio pack explains how to: recognize keys • analyze chord progressions • use the modes • play over nondiatonic harmony • use harmonic and melodic minor scales • use symmetrical scales such as chromatic, whole-tone and diminished scales • incorporate exotic scales such as Hungarian major and Gypsy minor • and much more!

00695563 Book/Online Audio $14.99

SPEED MECHANICS FOR LEAD GUITAR
INCLUDES TAB

Take your playing to the stratosphere with the most advanced lead book by this proven heavy metal author. *Speed Mechanics* is the ultimate technique book for developing the kind of speed and precision in today's explosive playing styles. Learn the fastest ways to achieve speed and control, secrets to make your practice time really count, and how to open your ears and make your musical ideas more solid and tangible. Packed with over 200 vicious exercises including Troy's scorching version of "Flight of the Bumblebee." Music and examples demonstrated on the accompanying online audio.

00699323 Book/Online Audio $19.99

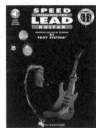

TOTAL ROCK GUITAR
INCLUDES TAB

A COMPLETE GUIDE TO LEARNING ROCK GUITAR

by Troy Stetina

This unique and comprehensive source for learning rock guitar is designed to develop both lead and rhythm playing. It covers: getting a tone that rocks • open chords, power chords and barre chords • riffs, scales and licks • string bending, strumming, palm muting, harmonics and alternate picking • all rock styles • and much more. The examples are in standard notation with chord grids and tab, and the audio includes full-band backing for all 22 songs.

00695246 Book/Online Audio $19.99

Visit Hal Leonard Online at
www.halleonard.com

Prices, contents, and availability subject to change without notice.

0418